Arras Counter-Attack
1940

Dedication
This book is dedicated to the soldiers of the Durham Light Infantry
and their successors in today's 'Rifles'.

Arras Counter-Attack
1940

Tim Saunders

Pen & Sword
MILITARY

First published in Great Britain in 2018 by
PEN AND SWORD MILITARY
an imprint of
Pen and Sword Books Ltd
47 Church Street
Barnsley
South Yorkshire S70 2AS

ISBN 978 1 47388 912 5

Printed and bound in England by
CPI Group (UK) Ltd, Croydon, CR0 4YY

Typeset in Times by CHIC GRAPHICS

Pen & Sword Books Ltd incorporates the imprints of
Pen & Sword Books Ltd incorporates the imprints of Pen & Sword
Archaeology, Atlas, Aviation, Battleground, Discovery,
Family History, History, Maritime, Military, Naval, Politics,
Railways, Select, Social History, Transport, True Crime,
Claymore Press, Frontline Books, Leo Cooper, Praetorian Press,
Remember When, Seaforth Publishing and Wharncliffe.

For a complete list of Pen and Sword titles please contact
Pen and Sword Books Limited
47 Church Street, Barnsley, South Yorkshire, S70 2AS, England
E-mail: enquiries@pen-and-sword.co.uk
Website: www.pen-and-sword.co.uk

Contents

Acknowledgements

In writing this book I am particularly indebted to my friend and colleague Richard Hone who not only made his extensive library of books on armour and the Durham Light Infantry available to me but provided some unique pictures, particularly those of the Experimental Mechanised Force. In a similar vein, my thanks and appreciation must go to Keith Brigstock, guardian of the Royal Artillery's living history, who not only introduced me to the Mark I 25-pounder gun but also to the works of 'Gun Buster' who, as an officer working under a pseudonym, left a detailed and revealing account of the Gunners' part in the 'Arras counter-attack'.

Regimental headquarters, their historians and museums have, as usual, helped significantly by providing the very necessary personal accounts and photographs for which I am exceedingly grateful.

As ever, the very existence of The National Archives and their most helpful staff was essential to this project. It is, however, clear that very few historians in general accounts of the campaign in specific chapters on the 'Arras counter-attack' have actually consulted the war diaries. These primary sources are, of course, important for a work looking at the operations of 21 May 1940 in detail.

Finally, as always, I am also most grateful to Matt Jones, Pamela Covey, Roni Wilkinson and Sylvia Menzies, the *Battleground* team with whom I have enjoyed working for more than fifteen years.

Tim Saunders
Warminster
November 2018

Introduction

'There was at the time, and there still is, some confusion of ideas about what is commonly known as the British "counter-attack" at Arras.' These words published in Major Ellis's *Official History of the 1940 Campaign* in 1953 still apply today! Was it a counter-attack or was it a limited clearance operation that simply ran into the flank of a panzer division? The essence of the continuing debate is that the operational and tactical aims south of Arras on 21 May 1940 were muddled and contradictory. Operationally, it was the beginning of the British part in a proposed Anglo-French counter-attack to sever the panzer corridor that ran north to the Channel, but tactically it was to secure Arras and gain 'elbow room' for a subsequent operation, i.e. the proposed counter-attack. That it ran into the flank of the 7th Panzer Division's infantry strung out in column of route was pure luck on the part of the British and the result of risk-taking on the part of Rommel.

Aside from the debate over what the 'Arras counter-attack' was or wasn't, this book is essentially about blitzkrieg, with an overview of the ten to twelve days that saw the Panzer Arm (*Panzerwaffe*) executing the 'sickle cut', as originally proposed by von Manstein, from the Ardennes across northern France in a 'decision-seeking' operation.

Blitzkrieg or 'Lightning War' was, however, in much of the German army of the 1930s a discredited concept, with the 1914 Schlieffen Plan that envisaged defeat of the French army within forty-two days being seen as the overambitious reason for Germany facing her geostrategic nightmare of a war on two fronts. Indeed, before the Second World War there are only a few occasions on which blitzkrieg can be found mentioned in any German military document or periodical. Many today, particularly in Germany, argue that blitzkrieg as an operational concept did not actually exist in the *Wehrmacht* in the late winter and early spring of 1940 and that the stunning victory in May/June of that year was brought about by circumstance rather than through a conscious strategic doctrine for the use of the new and very much still developing *Panzerwaffe*.

My aim in writing this book is to examine the battle in detail and get to the bottom of as many of the conflicting tales as possible to produce a balanced view of what actually happened. In addition, there is a battlefield tour instruction with not just a marked map but GPS-usable longitude and latitude to help navigation through the maze of villages in the Scarpe Valley and some that are now on the outer fringes of Arras.

I have also, with very scant information, tried my best to acknowledge the significant part played by French troops who fought among and alongside their Allies on 21 May 1940. British commentators often dismiss French participation as 'non-existent' or 'ineffective' when in fact it was neither. A lack of effective liaison is also blamed on the French but, of course, liaison is a two-way process and that it didn't happen is symptomatic of the disintegration of command structures, both British and French, rather than any wilful negligence that is often implied.

The correct terminology of the time for the Royal Tank Regiment (RTR) units and sub-units was 'battalion' and 'company'. I have, however, for the sake of clarity referred to RTR companies as 'squadrons' because with at various stages in the battle, infantry companies and the tanks being on the same ground along with a multiplicity of A, B and C companies is simply too confusing for the author, let alone the reader!

Again for clarity, I have referred to the main tanks used by the two Royal Tank Regiment battalions at Arras as the Mark I (Mk I) and the Mark II as the 'Matilda'. The proper designation for these tanks is Infantry Tank Matilda Mark I and Infantry Tank Matilda II.

Chapter 1

Between the Wars

The story of the development of armour in Europe during the interwar years is, of course, inseparable from the tactics put into effect by the Germans in May 1940. In this chapter the development of weapons, equipment and tactics between the final phase of the First World War and the retreat to Dunkirk is discussed.

The *Sostruppentactik* (Stormtrooper Tactics/Assault Team) of 1918, which embraced the technological developments and tactical lessons of the previous four years, produced a combined arms battle that was finally able to break the persistent state of trench-lock; this was the essence of blitzkrieg. These new tactics were certainly not confined to the Germans. For example, two operations conducted by the British Expeditionary Force (BEF) as the great German offensives of 1918 started to wane, demonstrate – albeit on a limited scale – the success of 'closely orchestrating' (General John Monash's description) the use of artillery, tanks, aircraft and infantry at Méteren (9th Scottish Division) and Le Hamel (Australian Corps). These operations were, of course, the prelude to the equally well-choreographed Battle of Amiens and the Hundred Days that

German stormtroopers in action during the Spring Offensives of 1918.

saw the Germans being driven back, in the case of some old Regular Army battalions of 1914 such as the 1st Dorsets, to within 10 miles of where it had all started at Mons.

As advocated by the then Colonel J.F.C. Fuller the previous year, the German and allied tactics of 1918 embraced the concept of speedy and deep penetration of enemy positions, by armour and mobile assault troops, heading for the opposing artillery, reserves and headquarters. In doing this they would aim to avoid areas of enemy resistance, leaving such places to be dealt with by the following infantry. Once out of range of artillery, close air support was to be relied upon to help sustain an advance, which would otherwise grind to a halt without fire support. Carrying tanks and the air-dropping of ammunition were also experimented with, as conventional waggons and limbers could only slowly make their way on destroyed roads and cross obstacles to reach the hitherto successful spearheads.

The seeds of what became known as blitzkrieg germinated on the Western Front in 1918 as doctrine increasingly advocated short bombardment, not to 'destroy' but stupefy, along with specially-armed, trained and equipped assault troops, who would move faster than enemy commanders, who were tied to telephone lines, could react and issue fresh orders.

If the war in 1918 showed all the signs of modernity, which had been learned at a great cost, the aftermath saw trench warfare and the whole First World War experience being regarded as an unpleasant aberration and, along with those 'nasty, dirty and unglamorous tanks', all to be forgotten as quickly as possible. There was little perceived need for the mobility, firepower and protection of the tank in any circumstance other than trench warfare and, as cavalrymen

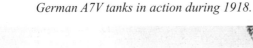

German A7V tanks in action during 1918.

pointed out, their arm had performed well with the resumption of open warfare in the final phase of the war. This process of denial was aided in the United Kingdom as the incomparable citizen armies of 1918 'melted away like spring snow' and the British Regular Army got back to 'real soldiering' on the North-West Frontier and war in Afghanistan in 1919.

André Maginot.

In France, despite the presence of armoured visionaries such as Colonel Charles de Gaulle, the lessons of the Verdun forts and a lingering belief in the superiority of the defensive brought about a ferro-concrete revival and the construction of the Maginot Line from 1930. In Germany, the armed forces emasculated by the hated Treaty of Versailles and the failure of the Schlieffen Plan to deliver victory similarly returned the majority of German military thought to pre-First World War levels.

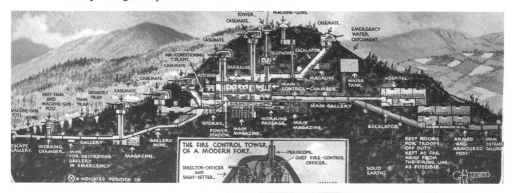

Maginot defences: the Maginot Line was a series of machine-gun, artillery and anti-tank casemates connected up by tunnels and served by troops in underground barracks.

In Britain, the Tank Design Department was closed in 1923 and the rusting hulks of redundant tanks were soon to be found in 'graveyards' around Bovington Camp in Dorset. Armoured development had been marginalized as the horse returned to the ascendancy. This, however, proved to be only temporary as mechanization was finally embraced by the British army but crucially, despite experiments, Britain lagged behind in the creation of tanks and armoured formations.

There were, of course, the British military philosophers, theorists and visionaries, many of whom had served as regular or wartime officers in the Tank Corps. More often than not, however, they were regarded as unwelcome zealots. This was particularly so in Britain, where not only had a pre-war military conservatism reasserted itself but there was a rolling policy of 'no war for ten years' which, in hindsight, we can see kept the need for armour at a comfortable distance.

In 1924 the Chief of the Imperial General Staff (CIGS), in a strategic study for the Chiefs of Staff Committee, wrote: 'I maintain that under existing world conditions we require no plans of campaign (except for small wars incidental to our Imperial position). There is no need to try to justify our existence by wasting our time and energies in the compilation of elaborate plans for wars against hypothetical enemies.'

His successor, in 1926, while recognizing that the army was now completely out of date, added that '…the war against Germany in 1914 was "abnormal"', and two years later said that it was 'wise to prepare an Expeditionary Force with a view to a war in Afghanistan'.

With the politicians reflecting the nation's 'never again' reaction to the First World War and, along with much of the army, appearing to be putting the clock back not merely to 1914 but to the nineteenth century, the Russian threat to India again received top priority.

Fuller and Liddell Hart
'Asses would rather have refuse than have gold.'
(Title page of Fuller's memoirs, quoting the Greek philosopher Herakleitos)
The two best-known British military theorists of the inter-war years were Captain Sir Basil Liddell Hart and Major General J.F.C. Fuller. Both had been developers and writers of tactics during the First World War and emerged post-war as advocates of mechanization and armour. They were backed up by a cadre of often equally unpopular Tank Corps officers such as Percy Hobart, who pressed for 'practical preparation (the adoption of armoured forces) for what a future war could bring'. Both Fuller and Liddell Hart retired in the 1920s to become journalists and writers on military affairs, some of which were translated into German.

One of the 'cadre of zealots' was General Martel, a Royal Engineer by trade who, as we will see, was to command the 50th Northumbrian Division at Arras in 1940. He had witnessed the debut of the tank on the Somme in September 1916 and had served as a junior officer on Fuller's staff, where he produced a service paper that, looking into the future, proposed a fully-armoured army. Despite military conservatism being in the ascendancy Martel, serving as a post-war major continued, as did many officers of the technical arms, to pursue his interest in armoured warfare. In short he joined the growing number of those who hotly debated, increasingly in print, the efficacy of armoured forces, their equipment and tactics.

Sir Basil Liddell Hart.

Major General J.F.C. Fuller.

The volume of similar writing from theorists across Europe, available in translation, provided food for thought to like-minded German officers who were contemplating their defeat and how to avoid it in the future. Building on the success of the *Sostruppentactik* of 1918, emerging German doctrinal ideas stressed attacking points of weakness, concentration of force and the all-important speed with which they could 'get inside the enemy's decision-making cycle'.

The extent to which British writers primed German thought is still debated but the works of Fuller, Liddell Hart, et al undoubtedly influenced the likes of Heinz Guderian, the 'father of the German Panzer Arm', the *Panzerwaffe*. Guderian's post-war career in the *Reichswehr* saw him as a member of the *Truppenamt* ('Troop Office'), a clandestine incarnation German General Staff that had been banned by the Treaty of Versailles. He went on in the late 1920s to lead the Centre for Army Transport and Motorised Tactics and was Chief of Staff of the Inspectorate of Motorised Troops in the early 1930s. Guderian studied the works of other writers and theorists extensively, including Brigadier Hobart who eventually commanded the first British permanently established tank brigade.

General Martel.

The young Heinz Guderian.

Above: Vickers MK II tanks and Carden Loyd carriers Nk IV. Left: The Brigade HQ command variant nicknamed 'Thunderbox' and a Vickers Mk IIB Light Tank.

Experimental Armoured Forces

Even though the British cavalry establishment was clinging to the horse, the tide of mechanization was flowing against them. In May 1927, a brigade-sized, fully-motorised, all-arms Experimental Mechanised Force (EMF) assembled at Tidworth on Salisbury Plain alongside 7 Infantry Brigade. It was originally to be commanded by General Fuller but having been refused additional specialist staff and resources, and believing all such refusals would inevitably lead to failure, he resigned. Brigadier Collins took command of the EMF in his place.

After a period of unit training and exercises with – for most of the men – unfamiliar vehicles and equipment, formation training began in mid-August, ranging across the rolling Salisbury Plain, ideal for armour and mechanized troops. The type of exercises conducted ranged from simple attack, defence and counter-attack through to the complex operation of an assault river crossing, which had been considered impossible by critics. These still small-scale exercises in crossing the River Avon and the faux crossing in the Berril Valley, overseen by umpires, were regarded as a success, even if 2 Somerset Light Infantry in trucks were unable to keep up with the tracked vehicles across country. Recommendations, however, for a tracked armoured personnel carrier that could keep up with tanks were firmly rejected on grounds of cost.

In short, the results achieved by the EMF during two years of increasingly complex but relatively small-scale exercises proved that a balanced force of tanks, mobile infantry and artillery, plus other supporting arms, worked well. As a result, numerous papers and reports were circulating and beginning to change minds, not all of them British!

As an example of the thought and activity brought about by this experimentation, we return to Martel: he was responsible for the single-man tankette, the prototype of which he built himself during 1925. This machine spawned test vehicles and a derivative tankette built by Carden Loyd. The concept of a single crewman in a recce tank was not a success but his experiments gave birth to the light tank, the successors of which were among the British armoured fighting vehicles at Arras in 1940. Martel's other ventures were the result of his engineering background, one of which while stationed with a company of Royal Engineers at Tidworth on Salisbury Plain was to help the Experimental Mechanised Force with bridging techniques. As a result, he developed plans for an early hydraulically-launched armoured bridge-layer.

Despite the success of the armoured experiments on

Percy Hobart: in 1934 he became commander of the first permanent armoured brigade and Inspector Royal Tank Corps.

Uttrappe armoured reconnaissance vehicle (1931) as permitted by the Treaty of Versailles.

Salisbury Plain, at a time when the world was sliding into depression, the natural democratic inclination for butter over guns and with Britain being still firmly in the shadow of the First World War, the Experimental Mechanised Force was disbanded. The EMF was dispersed and the British army took another developmental line and considered raising tank brigades, with which came the practice of forming ad hoc grouping of tanks and infantry for particular operations rather than following the example of the EMF and having formations that were properly trained and equipped for armoured warfare. This practice was to fail at Arras so obviously in 1940 and was, arguably, with tank brigades in the order of battle, still being overcome during 1944. In Normandy all too often the British infantry formations and armour were on the same battlefield but usually fighting their own separate battles with only cursory coordination.

Meanwhile, in Germany a still marginal but nonetheless active development programme of armoured forces was under way which, as in Britain, was far from universally popular. It was also, of course, being undertaken in the shadow of the Treaty of Versailles restrictions. Having monitored the reports, articles and pamphlets, such as the remarkable *Provisional Regulations Part II* emanating from the British Experimental Mechanised Force, Guderian, often paying for translations himself, proposed the raising of German armoured divisions in the 1920s. This too was rejected but with a new Inspector of Motorised Forces, General Lutz, taking post in 1931, two years later the concept was gaining wider support. With Hitler in the Reich's Chancellery bent on revenge and intending to re-arm Germany when the moment was right, the formation of the first three panzer divisions was finally ordered in October 1935. The *Panzerwaffe* who, less than five years later, would deliver the 1940 blitzkrieg, was born.

The lightly armed Panzer IB was only intended for development and training but like many obsolescent AFVs became a use as platforms for other weapons and equipment.

Development of the *Panzerwaffe*

Much of the early development had necessarily been conducted in secret, as the trials moved from armoured trucks to mock tanks and eventually to the 'experimental' Panzer Is and Panzer IIs. A significant part of German trials and development work was conducted away from Western diplomats' gaze in Russia. Hitler's temporary marriage of convenience with the politically polar opposite Soviet Union was from the outset a great advantage. Meanwhile, back in Germany dummy tanks were on show to calm the fears of defence attachés and increasingly nervous governments in Paris and London.

The tactical doctrine of the *Panzerwaffe* was initially based on the British 1927 *Provisional Instructions on Tank and Armoured Car Training*; another product of the Experimental Mechanised Force. German armoured commanders preferred these instructions over those of the French, who saw the tank as being deployed and operating in support of the infantry. This German decision was very important for the future development of the Panzer Arm (*Panzerwaffe*) into an all-arms grouping around the tank. This gave the panzers a far greater freedom of action and allowed a distinctly German doctrine of armoured warfare to be developed and put into practice. It was not only that this direction took German armoured doctrine way beyond the concepts envisaged by Germany's potential enemies in the mid-1930s. Under Hitler the Germans, from lagging behind in the development of armoured warfare during the First World War and its aftermath, by the late thirties had the *Panzerwaffe* leading the way and laying the foundations for a stunning blitzkrieg in the summer of 1940.

As war clouds gathered, resulting from Hitler's repeated risk-taking from reoccupation of the Rhineland onwards, a second batch of panzer divisions started to be formed from other motorized troops in 1937/8. The 4th and 5th

A Panzer IV and a Czech M35 (t) on pre-war German manoeuvres. The white band on the NCO's helmet denotes an umpire.

Panzer II.

Panzer divisions were fully-fledged armoured formations, while the 1st and 2nd Light Divisions were copies of the French divisions Légère Mécanique. Following indifferent performance in Poland in 1939, in early 1940 these divisions became the fully-fledged 6th and 7th Panzer Divisions, as did the forming 3rd and 4th Light Divisions, which quickly became the 8th and 9th Panzer Divisions. The final armoured formation in the German 1940 order of battle was the 10th Panzer Division which, still forming, had been in reserve during the Polish campaign.

The Czech crises of 1938/39, at a time when the vast majority of panzers were training and development vehicles, brought the *Panzerwaffe* a shot in the arm in the form of the Czech 35(t) and 38(t) tanks, which were broadly comparable to the German Pz IIIs and Pz IVs. Not only that, the Czech production facilities were also in German hands and in the 1940 campaign 325 of these tanks were available, with Rommel's 7th Panzer Division's tank fleet, for instance, being almost entirely made up of Czech 38(t) tanks.

Czech 38(t) tank and accompanying infantry.

By the time of the campaign in the West the panzer troops were backed up by ten motorized divisions, which together with the panzers provided almost unrivalled mobility and punch to the *Wehrmacht*. Thanks to their concentration into a critical mass, German armour was able to defeat the French army and the BEF, who together possessed a greater number of tanks of an arguably better quality.

The Outbreak of War

In the early summer of 1939, before the outbreak of war, Hitler told his generals that '…war with England now would be tantamount to the end of Germany'. That Germany went to war shortly afterwards was the result of 'foreign policy accident and extreme adventurism on the part of Hitler'. His catalogue of risk-taking since 1933 and the lack of substantive response by his neighbours makes unedifying reading in France and Britain and largely accounts for Hitler's growing adventurism.

> March 1935: Hitler reintroduced compulsory military service in violation of the Treaty of Versailles; the Western powers reacted only weakly.
> March 1936: German troops reoccupied the Rhineland; the Western powers only protested.
> September 1938: During the Munich Conference Hitler demanded that the German parts of Czechoslovakia should be ceded to Germany; the Allies submitted.
> March 1939: The *Wehrmacht* occupied the non-German Czech provinces of Moravia and Bohemia; again very little was done.

Adolf Hitler.

Hitler, however, overreached himself when he invaded Poland. The Reich's Chancellery's chief translator Paul Schmidt recalled the reaction in Hitler's office to his translation of the British declaration of war:

> After I finished, there was total silence...Hitler sat there as if petrified and stared straight ahead. He was not stunned, as was maintained later, and he did not rant and rave either as some have claimed they knew. He sat in his seat completely quiet and motionless. After a while that seemed like an eternity to me, he turned to Ribbentrop who remained standing at a window as if frozen. 'What now?' Hitler asked the Foreign Minister with a furious gaze in his eye as if he was indicating that Ribbentrop had misinformed him about the reaction of the British. Softly Ribbentrop replied: 'I assume that the French will shortly give us an identical ultimatum' ... Göring turned to me and said 'If we lose this war, may Heaven have mercy on us!

Hitler's miscalculation in his invasion of Poland pitched Germany into war with Europe's two strongest naval, military and economic powers, no less than three to five years before his own armed forces believed that they would be ready for renewed war. His adventurism led his country once again into a full-blown world war for which he had no plan or strategy; 'Hitler the gambler had played a very bad hand and had lost!' To make matters worse, Germany's military operations during the second half of the 1930s had been barely-opposed annexation operations, although the German armed forces did have some small practical experience gained during the Spanish Civil War. In Poland, however, they were about to gain much more experience.

The Lessons of Poland
The five-week campaign in Poland was not straightforward for the Germans, who fought a costly and overall operationally conventional campaign that required almost the entire *Wehrmacht* along with Soviet forces from the east to completely overcome the Poles. This was the case, even though the Poles had an old-fashioned armed force and a command structure and mentality that were no longer fit for purpose. Not only that, by the end of the campaign Germany had all but run out of ammunition and other combat supplies to sustain immediate operations.

Major all-arms exercises had been planned for August 1939 but had been cancelled due to Hitler's adventure in the east. Consequently, the Polish campaign was the first time that German armour and aircraft had worked together on any significant scale. This is a measure of just how far Germany was from a coherent, practical implementation of the doctrine that the likes of Guderian had been developing. At this point, the stunning success of operations in the west in 1940 just seven months later would have seemed illusory.

The invasion of Poland in September 1939. Above: SS motorcycle troops still wearing First World War helmets.

Even though German armour in Poland had predominantly operated conventionally, tactically, numerous practical lessons were learned across the *Panzerwaffe* regarding the difficulties of armoured warfare and how to overcome them. At the operational level, General Guderian and the other advocates of armoured warfare were, however, able to point to the effect of a relatively small group of panzers of the 2nd (Wien) Panzer Division. They found a lightly-defended section of thickly-wooded ridge, attacked through it and enveloped a major enemy force holding the Jablunka Pass.

Rommel and Hitler, Poland 1939.

Among those impressed by the *Panzerwaffe* was infantryman *Generalmajor* Erwin Rommel, one of Hitler's favourites and commander of the *Führerbegleitbrigade* (Führer Escort Brigade) during the 1939 campaign. Of particular note was his grasping of the essence of armoured warfare and the ability of panzers, as described above, to infiltrate around enemy positions, which in turn was to become his own trademark. From a conservative rejectionist, overnight he became a devotee of the panzer, so much so that he engineered his appointment to the command of the 7th Panzer Division as it converted to a full-blown panzer formation in early 1940.

It is also worth noting that *Generalfeldmarschall* Keitel (Head of *Oberkommando der Wehrmacht*, the *OKW*, Supreme Command of the Armed Forces) said 'a French attack during the Polish Campaign would have encountered only a German screen, not a real defence.' Arguably a French attack aimed at the Ruhr – Germany's military powerhouse – would have concluded matters rapidly. This state of affairs further highlights Germany's lack of preparedness for full-scale war, as much as events in Poland. Hitler, however, went on to astound his generals in October 1939, before the Polish campaign was over, by announcing his intent to launch an immediate attack on the West.

Chapter 2

The Development of *Fall Gelb*

The Germans may have had the tools at the operational level in the form of the *Panzerwaffe* with which to execute a blitzkrieg, but in most of the German army 'lightning war' languished firmly in the long shadow cast by the failure of the Schlieffen Plan and defeat in 1918.

Despite the generals' protests at the impossibility of an attack on France in late 1939, fearing a rapid Allied build-up in the West, Hitler insisted and *Oberkommando der Heeres* (*OKH*, Army Supreme Command) rushed to produce plans for an attack at the earliest opportunity. However, for a variety of reasons, principally weather, the attack on the West was delayed no fewer than twenty-nine times. These repeated postponements allowed time for a rapid expansion of the *Wehrmacht* during the 'Phoney War' between October 1939 and May 1940. During this period Germany not only replaced her losses in Poland but German industry even outstripped the feared build-up of British and French forces.

Crucially, over winter the German tank fleet of the Polish campaign, predominantly Panzer Is and IIs with a mere handful of heavier Mk IIIs and IVs, was increased; the number of Panzer IIIs had quadrupled to 785 vehicles and Panzer IVs had more than doubled to 290. In addition, the number of Czech tanks (M-35(t) and M38(t)) available rose to a total of 380. This increase was generally reflected across the range of equipment types and ammunition natures, which had sunk to critical levels by the end of the Polish campaign.

Early Plans for the Invasion of the West

'When France lay prostate under the German heel, the men of the victorious army would have been astonished had they known that their highest military chiefs had not believed such a victory to be possible – and that victory had been gained by a plan which had been forced on a doubting General Staff as a result of a back door approach.'

(Liddell Hart)

The initial German plans for the invasion of the West were initially limited and conventional, in contrast with the far-reaching decision-seeking nature of the Schlieffen Plan. In fact, a similar decisive blitzkrieg was far from the minds of

Panzer IIIE command vehicle with a frame antenna.

Panzer IV. In updated versions the Pz IV remained in production until the end of the war.

the *OKH* during the winter of 1939/40. Once again their plan was based on a violation of Belgian neutrality, thereby avoiding the Maginot Line defences on the common Franco/German border south of Luxembourg. In this plan, however, rather than swinging in a south-westerly direction to envelop the French, the German armies, it proposed, would break through and head north-west for the Channel coast; a limited aim, with a protracted struggle ensuing.

The first *Führerbefehl* (Führer Order) No. 6 on the subject of the invasion of the West was issued on 9 October 1939:

> An offensive will be planned on the northern flank of the Western Front, through Luxembourg, Belgium and Holland. This offensive must be launched at the earliest moment possible and in the greatest strength possible.
>
> The purpose of this offensive will be the defeat of as much possible of the French Army and the allied forces fighting on their side, and concurrently to capture as much territory as possible in Holland, Belgium and Northern France to act as a base for the successful conduct of the air and sea war against England and as a wide protective area for the economically vital Ruhr.

In other words, there was no intent or expectation that this plan for <u>initial</u> action in the West would knock France out of the war. Rather it would be the first step in what was expected to be a protracted struggle in the style of the First World War, lacking an early strategic decision.

The first unambitious draft of the operational plan, *Fall Gelb* (Case Yellow/Manstein Plan), with the *schwerpunkt* (main effort) lying firmly in the north with Army Group B, was rejected by Hitler, despite its close adherence to his *führerbefehl*. There followed a protracted period of revision, further revision and resulting uncertainty born of repeated tinkering until the weather finally deteriorated sufficiently to make operations impractical.

Meanwhile, the Chief of Staff of General von Rundstedt's Army Group A, *Generalleutnant* Erich von Manstein, had been equally unimpressed with the orders

Erich von Manstein.

emanating from Berlin that had repeatedly arrived on his headquarters desk at Koblenz. His chief concern was that *Fall Gelb* would commit German forces to a head-on clash with the strongest Allied armies in the north, which would naturally limit the chances of success. His counter-proposal, which first saw the light of day in late October 1939 and later became known as Operation *Sichelschnitt* (Sickle Cut), saw the *schwerpunkt* being moved south to Army Group A, where panzer divisions would slice through the supposedly

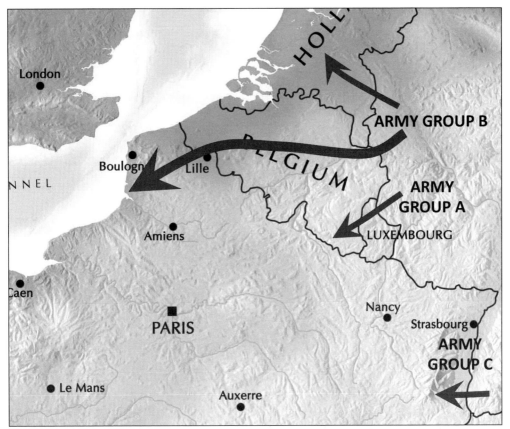

Fall Gelb *original plan.*

impenetrable Ardennes, cross a lightly-defended stretch of the River Meuse at Sedan and head for the Channel coast enveloping and, in the process, cutting off the northern Allied armies. Meanwhile, once across the Meuse a secondary force would strike south into the area that von Manstein estimated the French would designate as their assembly area for the inevitable counterstroke.

Manstein proposed that, at the culmination of a successful armoured strike to the coast, a second *sichelschnitt*, this time to the south, would follow. This concept was formulated with the informal assistance of General Guderian's armoured expertise. Fortuitously, Guderian's Headquarters XIX Panzer Corps was also located in Koblenz; this plan would meet Hitler's revised requirement of maximum destruction of enemy formations, plus a maximum gain of territory, while avoiding a head-on collision of *schwerpunkts*.

Issued with the approval of von Rundstedt, initially von Manstein's plan was dismissed and derided by the *OKH* as an 'egocentric plan to give Army Group A greater importance' and was not forwarded to the *OKW* or to Hitler. Von Rundstedt, however, persisted in his attempts to bring the 'Manstein Plan' to the attention of the *OKW* and the Führer. In the meantime, General Halder,

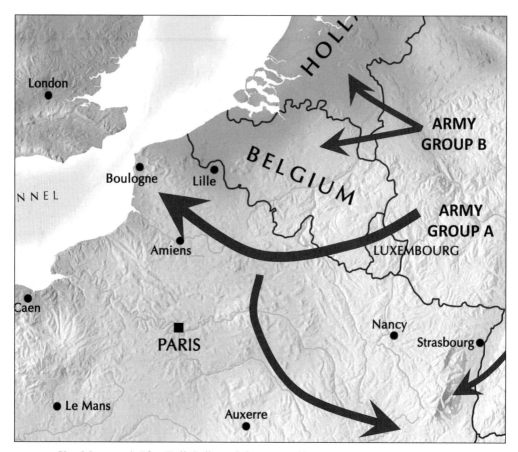

Von Manstein's Plan Fall Gelb *and the two sickle cuts.*

who could do little about von Rundstedt, ensured that von Manstein, who he regarded as 'a busy and annoying beaver', was promoted out of the way to the command of a new corps forming in the east. Alistair Horne summed up the situation when he wrote 'the cautious Halder clearly evidenced resentment towards the daring genius of Manstein'.

General Franz Halder.

Meanwhile, Hitler, during his repeated interference and direction of *Fall Gelb*'s planning had also, and separately, come up with the idea of attacking through the Ardennes. This unformed tactical concept, again fortuitously, coincided with Halder at last beginning to see merit in von Manstein's proposals. At the same time, a key moment when Hitler's instinctive inclination and von Manstein's professional plan started to come together was during a staff visit to a war game exercise held at Headquarters Army Group A. Some of the Führer's personal staff who attended were immediately struck by the proposal and the way it could put their master's instinct into practice.

Halder (far right), Hitler and his staff.

Even though Hitler did not like von Manstein, when the latter reported to
Berlin prior to taking up his corps command, the general was listened to in
unusual silence by the Führer as he outlined his far-reaching operational plan
during a private audience on 17 February. Hitler was convinced by this solution,
which greatly exceeded his hitherto purely tactical level thoughts of attacking
through the Ardennes. The die was cast and a fourth major recast of the *Fall
Gelb* plan was issued, with both Hitler and Halder increasingly attempting to
take credit for von Manstein's concept, the former becoming convinced that
von Manstein was the only one of the generals who understood <u>his</u> plan!

Contrary to the oft-cited case, the loss of a set of the third iteration of *Fall
Gelb* plans was not the reason for the switch of *schwerpunkt* south to von
Rundstedt's Army Group. A *Luftwaffe* staff officer accepted a lift in a friend's
aircraft, which became lost in bad weather and was forced to land in neutral
Belgium at Mechelen. The two officers attempted to burn the plans but failed
and the Allies were, of course, informed of the contents of the scorched remains
by the Belgians. The Allies had, however, reacted strongly to the incident,
deploying their troops and in doing so very clearly indicated that the BEF, in
company with the First and Seventh French armies would advance to the River
Dyle when Belgian neutrality was violated and the Belgian government

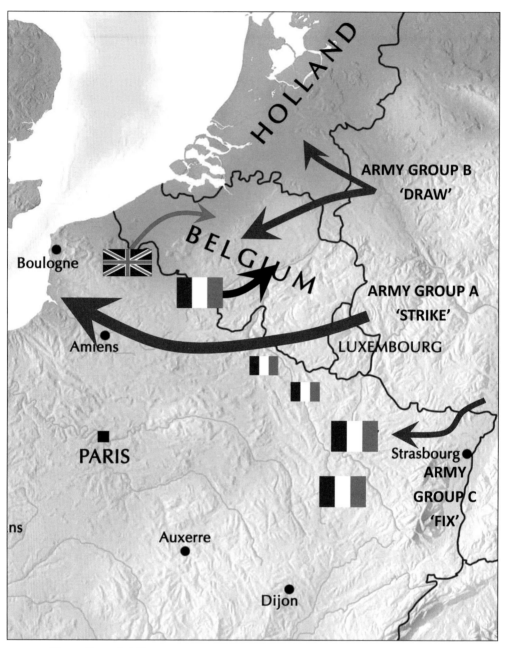

Draw, fix and strike.

requested help. Once calm had been restored, the French assumed that the Mechelen incident was an attempt at a double bluff and that there was, therefore, no need to change Allied plans.

The operational plan outlined by von Manstein in October went through considerable development and refinement, not to say argument, before it reached its final form for the offensive in May 1940. In *Fall Gelb*'s development the Germans were aided by their knowledge of the Allied intent to abandon the fortifications on the Franco/Belgian border, which they had been labouring on since the autumn, when the German attack on the West began. The German intent, when the Allied armies advanced to the Dyle Line, was for Army Group B to draw and fix or tie the Allies down in battle in central Belgium. To aid this, operations in the north by Army Group B were to be portrayed as the German *schwerpunkt*, being supported by *fallschirmjäger* (paratroopers), three panzer divisions and other motorized troops to help the illusion. The Germans' aim was to suck the northern Allied armies deep into a 'revolving door' trap.

Meanwhile, amid a news blackout Army Group A was preparing to strike through the Ardennes across the River Meuse and on into northern France, just as von Manstein envisaged. The smaller Army Group C was to fix French forces and similarly divert attention away from the central front with their attack on the Maginot Line.

The 'Sickle Cut' Plan

That the 'forested hill and narrow defiles' of the Ardennes were impenetrable to any large force was axiomatic as far as the French military was concerned but Fuller on a cycling holiday found that this was far from the case. There was a good road network, with a substantial amount of open ground and quite practicable for armour. A French deputy – a politician, not a soldier – was similarly convinced and his report, plus any other that dared to suggest that the Ardennes was anything but impenetrable, was overclassified and thus deeply buried.

In planning their offensive, the Germans had, of course, the attacker's prerogative of selecting the where, the when and the how much. They were thus able to ensure a significant superiority of numbers in the sector selected for the *schwerpunkt*, while the Allies had, in addition to delivering their own Dyle Plan, a long front to hold.

Von Rundstedt, Commander Army Group A.

Consequently, as the *Fall Gelb schwerpunkt*, Army Group A had grouped under it the Fourth, Twelfth and Sixteenth armies, along with Panzer Group Kleist with a total of forty-five divisions, seven of which were panzer divisions. Second and Ninth armies were to follow as a second echelon. In the Ardennes the Belgians had but two divisions, while the French intended on the outbreak of war to send four light cavalry divisions into the Belgian Ardennes, along with a pair of cavalry brigades (all of these were light armoured forces). The Meuse itself, north of the Maginot Line facing Army Group A, was held by seven mostly second-rate divisions with no immediately available reserve formations. So confident were the French that the Ardennes was impassable they were happy with the defensive arrangements, believing that if a force did by some chance attack at Sedan, that they would have plenty of time to react. They estimated that it would take a force a minimum of five days to fight their way through the Ardennes and would not be strong enough to mount an attack across the Meuse until the tenth to fourteenth day of the offensive.

Von Kleist.

The key element of the German plan was the massing of the panzers and motorized troops into Panzer Group Kleist. This army-sized formation consisting of Panzer Corps Guderian (XIX Corps: three panzer divisions), Panzer Corps Reinhart (XXXI Corps: two panzer and two motorised infantry divisions) and Motorised Corps Wietersheim (XVI Corps: one panzer and a motorized infantry division) was a temporary expedient. Panzer Group Kleist's northern flank would be protected by Panzer Corps Hoth with a pair of panzer divisions.

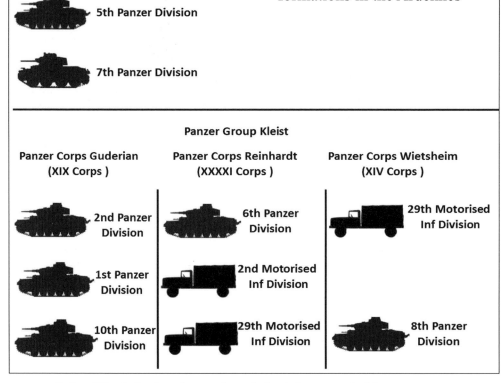

Order of Battle for the advance through the Ardennes to the Meuse.

Rommel supervising the training of the 7th Panzer Division on the River Moselle in Germany during early 1940.

The German use of *gruppe* or group normally indicates a temporary grouping of forces under a nominated commander for a specific task. In this case, so opposed were the mass of senior German officers to the fourth iteration of *Fall Gelb* – in particular to the plans that von Kleist and Guderian were developing in detail to negotiate the defiles of the Ardennes – that a deal was made. Its essence was that if the panzers became bogged down by Franco-Belgian delaying operations or failed to cross the Meuse (as was expected by many) and the infantry caught up with them, they would be taken under command of the three armies and operations would continue on more conventional lines thereafter. The clear and absolute intent of Generals von Kleist and Guderian was to keep ahead of the slower-moving infantry in order to preserve and demonstrate the capability of the *Panzerwaffe*. This overwhelming need for speed and von Manstein's imaginative plan were the foundations of the German victory and what became known as blitzkrieg.

In cutting across the rear of the northern Allied armies in the dash to the Channel, the aim of the concept initiated by von Manstein was nothing less than the *Panzerwaffe* producing a decisive operation that would avoid protracted First World War-like battle on a long front.

Panzer Group von Kleist

Oberst Karl-Heinz Frieser defined blitzkrieg as a method of '…concentrated employment of armour and air forces to confuse the enemy with speed and surprise and to encircle him, after successful breakthrough, by means of far-reaching thrusts. The objective is to defeat the enemy quickly in a decision-seeking action.'

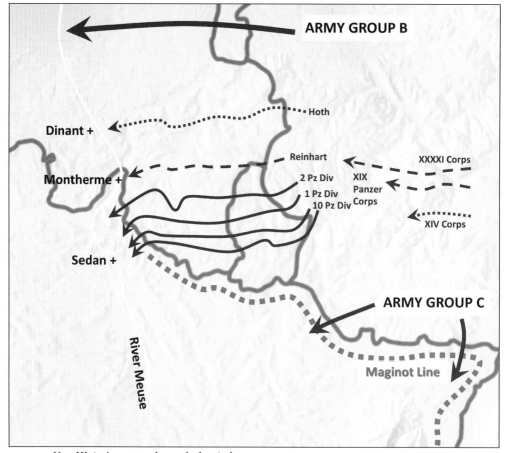

Von Kleist's routes through the Ardennes.

To cover the 110 miles of narrow roads and defiles from the German border through the Ardennes to the 80-yard-wide River Meuse at Sedan in seventy-two hours was the aim; any longer and the operation was likely to be compromised and give the French sufficient time to reinforce the defences around Sedan. Even the prospect of the panzer divisions becoming stuck in stultifying traffic jams on the four available roads, predicted even by von Rundstedt's new chief of staff, caused Guderian to waver. However, detailed planning and the insistence on speed, at almost all costs, in training left the *panzertruppen* in no doubt as to what was required of them: to reach the Meuse within three days.

Fall Gelb

The code word 'Danzig' for the execution of *Fall Gelb* was finally given at 2100 hours on 9 May 1940 and at 0435 the following morning Panzer Group Kleist crossed the border into the Ardennes. H-Hour closely coordinated with the capture of the Belgian border fortification further north by the *fallschirmjäger* (see Battleground *Fort Eben Emael*).

With XIX Panzer Corps leading, with a less than favourable allocation of routes for the panzers and the resulting tens of miles of traffic jams on the roads and tracks through the Ardennes, Guderian drove his divisions on, earning the nickname 'Schnell (Fast) Heinz'. This was exactly what had been inculcated in his officers and men during months of training, the aim being not only to reach the Meuse before the French could react but to stay well ahead of the infantry division and subordination to them. Unencumbered by a more conventional approach, von Kleist, Guderian and their officers believed that only this would give the *Panzerwaffe* the opportunity to deliver that decision-making operation.

Their first objective was the Meuse at Sedan 12 miles north of the end of the Maginot Line. Convinced of the impossibility of armour striking through the Ardennes, here the French had deployed third-rate troops to cover the river barrier, not in underground fortresses of a Maginot type but in surface concrete bunkers, many of which were still under construction or awaiting commissioning. Even so, the risks involved in an opposed river crossing were formidable and much of Army Group A believed it to be beyond the capabilities of panzer divisions.

The first spearheads of the three panzer divisions reached the hills above the Meuse on the afternoon of 12 May, well within the proscribed seventy-two hours, having carved their way through the Belgian Chasseurs des Ardennes and six delaying positions manned by French light armoured formations, plus the *Maison Fortifiée* line just inside the French frontier. Guderian issued his preliminary orders for the assault crossing between 1835 and 1930, with confirmatory orders being issued at 0830 hours the following morning.

The French had believed that it would take the Germans five days to penetrate the series of delaying positions and a further five to nine days to get

Guderian's command post. The three signallers are using an Enigma machine.
Vehicle Sd.Kfz.251/6. Note the 'bedstead' on frame antenna.

sufficient resources through the Ardennes and assembled before they could consider an opposed assault crossing; plenty of time to redeploy against what was considered to be an unlikely eventuality anyway.

The operation to force the Meuse began at 0800 hours the following day with the full might of the *Luftwaffe* in support, stunning the low-grade French troops of the 55th Division, positioned in often incomplete concrete bunkers. By nightfall, despite some difficulties, the exhausted panzer grenadiers of all three divisions were across the Meuse and had secured a bridgehead over one of Europe's greatest waterways. The part played by the *Luftwaffe* during 13 May in its rolling raids as flying artillery is hard to overestimate, particularly as much of the panzer divisions' artillery was still struggling through the Ardennes traffic jams.

During the night of 13 May and into the following day, ferrying and bridging operations were under way with Allied aircraft attempting to destroy the vital

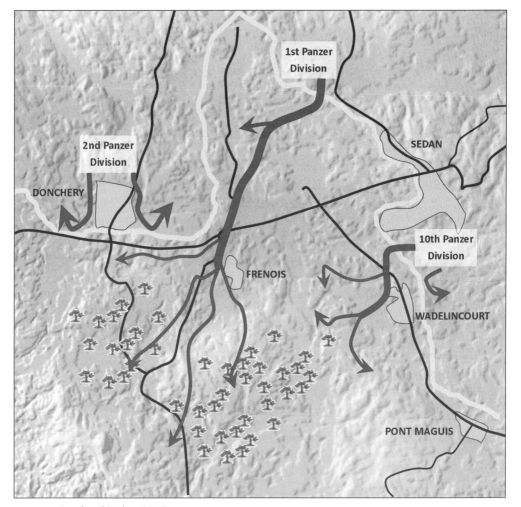

Battle of Sedan 1940.

crossings, having to repeatedly brave walls of anti-aircraft fire. The panzers, however, started to cross at 1600 hours on 14 May as the French command and control system started to crumble and by that evening the Germans had their breakthrough.

The French had deployed forces to attempt to contain and destroy the rapidly-expanding German bridgehead but by the time they had reacted it was too late. The resulting three-day pitched armoured battle around the hilltop village of Stonne on the southern flank of the break-out is an example of what could have happened in a clash of *schwerpunkts* that the original *Fall Gelb* plan envisaged and reinforces even further the brilliance of Manstein's idea to strike through the Ardennes towards a weak point in the French defences.

Panzer Corps Hoth

Meanwhile, further north, by 15 May the 6th Panzer Division (XXXI Panzer Corps, Reinhardt) had also unexpectedly crossed the Meuse at Monthermé and was making spectacular progress west but we must direct our attention 20 miles further north to Hoth's Panzer Corp (XV) and *Generalmajor* Rommel's 7th Panzer Divisions. This corps was to operate on von Kleist's right flank and in cutting through the northern part of the Ardennes, Hoth's task was to protect Guderian's main armoured punch. With his corps consisting of two panzer divisions, the 5th and 7th, General Hermann Hoth also believed that speed was the key to covering the 70 miles to the Meuse and crossing it before the Ninth French Army could be directed south to counter-attack. In Rommel, the *Panzerwaffe*'s armoured convert, he found an excellent executioner of his plans.

General Hermann Hoth.

From the outset of the campaign, Rommel and his panzers began gaining the nickname the 'Ghost Division' because of Rommel's intuitive ability to find gaps in enemy positions, slip through them ghost-like and attack them in the rear. So fast was Rommel's progress towards the Meuse that Hoth placed the advance guard of the 5th Panzer Division under his command, as the remainder of that division was strung out well to the rear on what was an open flank. Thus it was that a company of panzers from *Oberst* Werner's 31st Panzer Regiment (5th Panzer Division) were the first Germans to reach the banks of the Meuse at 1645 hours. Even though they were temporarily under his command, they were technically not, as Rommel later wrote, 'his troops' and the first German troops across the river were a company of the 5th Panzer Division's 8th Motor Cycle Battalion, which was a part of Werner's *kampfgruppe*. Such minor details have rarely stood in the way of an accomplished self-publicist like Rommel.

The afternoon had seen leading elements of *Kampfgruppe* Werner attempting to reach bridges before they were blown and in one case having a bridge demolished under a pair of armoured cars while in the act of capturing it. It looked as if attempts to secure a crossing had failed but during the night motor cycle patrols spotted an unguarded weir and shortly after dark on 12 May slipped across, first onto an island and then over an unblown weir and lock onto the enemy bank. A small bridgehead under fire from French artillery was in place by 2300 hours.

During the night of 12/13 May two French formations started to arrive on the west bank of the Meuse, the 5th Motorised and 18th Infantry divisions. As a result of poor coordination there was a gap between the two divisions near the weir, which enabled Werner's men to reinforce the motor-cycle troops and a useful bridgehead to be established. By 0530 hours on 13 May, no less than three infantry battalions of the 5th Panzer Division were across the river, with a panzer company on the home bank in support.

Even with the lucky break of a weir and lock and a small bridgehead, Rommel had to face the prospect of an assault crossing of the Meuse at two separate points in the face of the 18th French Infantry Division. This of course was without the prodigious support of the *Luftwaffe* afforded to the XIX Panzer Corps as the air arm's *schwerpunkt* was further north during 13 May.

Arriving at the Meuse, Rommel had issued his well-exercised and pre-prepared orders for the two crossings. One adjacent to the 5th Panzer's

The weir and lock on the River Meuse near Houx.

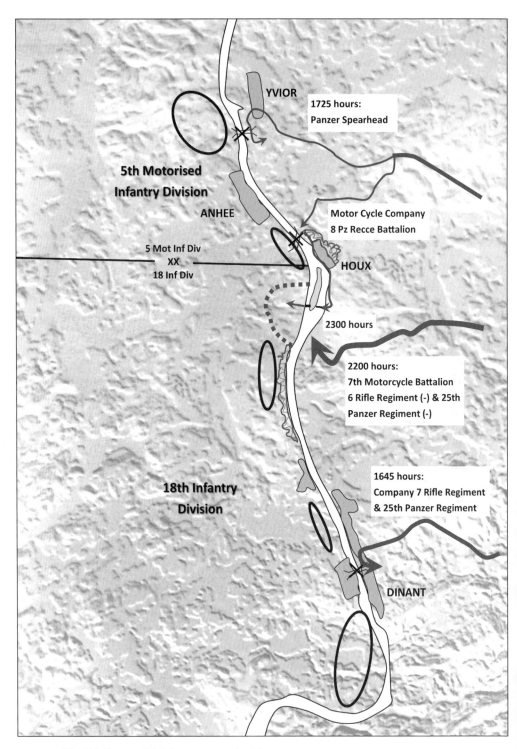

YVIOR

1725 hours:
Panzer Spearhead

5th Motorised
Infantry Division

ANHEE

Motor Cycle Company
8 Pz Recce Battalion

5 Mot Inf Div
XX
18 Inf Div

HOUX

2300 hours

2200 hours:
7th Motorcycle Battalion
6 Rifle Regiment (-) & 25th
Panzer Regiment (-)

1645 hours:
Company 7 Rifle Regiment
& 25th Panzer Regiment

18th Infantry
Division

DINANT

The 7th Panzer Division crosses the Meuse.

bridgehead was to be led by his 7th Motor Cycle Battalion followed by the 6th Rifle Regiment and the second several miles upstream, north of Dinant, by the 7th Rifle Regiment. Both crossings were quickly in trouble with plunging fire from the cliffs and buildings taking a heavy toll on the German infantry and engineers paddling the rubber boats. Defeat stared the 7th Panzer in the face but Rommel, reverting to the type that had earned him the Pour le Mérite during the First World War, laboured tirelessly in the front line siting individual weapons and leading from the front in exactly the same way that we will see him in action at Arras a week later. Seemingly against the odds Rommel succeeded in securing a shallow bridgehead north of Dinant.

During the course of the following day on 14 May, Rommel's persistence eventually broke the 18th Division's resistance opposite him and he drove his men on to success. If Guderian's success at Sedan was spectacular, Rommel's

7th Panzer division's pioneers (engineers) ferrying an armoured car (Sd.Kfz.221) across the Meuse.

performance – even allowing for some exaggeration and credit-taking – in far from ideal conditions and with little external support against far higher quality troops was stellar.

Further north 5th Panzer had advanced from their overnight bridgehead and borne the brunt of the French counter-attacks from the north. Hoth's bridgehead across the Meuse at the end of the day had been expanded to a depth of 2 miles and a breadth of a similar distance.

Break-Out

'And then what are you going to do?' was Hitler's question when Guderian had explained in the Chancellery his leading part in the timetable to cross the Meuse. According to Guderian, he replied that he should head for Antwerp or Paris as directed but best of all head for Abbeville and the Channel coast. No firm direction was, however, given but every commander in the XIX Panzer Corps knew that the English Channel was their objective. By contrast, Hitler and virtually the entire military establishment believed that even if von Kleist managed to cross the Meuse, operations would proceed along more conventional lines with the infantry divisions. Guderian had other ideas for XIX Panzer Corps!

Having successfully crossed the Meuse, risking the possibility of an early French counter-attack by the Second Army from the south and with the vital bridge over the Ardennes Canal at Malmy in his hands, rather than awaiting the arrival of the rest of Army Group A, on the afternoon of 14 May Guderian disobeyed orders. He believed that the ponderous French command system was incapable of reacting to the previous day's crossing of the Meuse in a timely manner and therefore took a risk. The 1st and 2nd Panzer divisions charged 25 miles west to Rethel, leaving the 10th Panzer Division and the *Grossdeutschland* Regiment to expand and secure the bridgehead awaiting the motorized infantry of *Panzergruppe* Kleist. In his memoirs Guderian said of his actions that day: 'The essence of the success at Sedan is not to be found in the breakthrough action as such but rather in the immediate exploitation of the breakthrough by the thrust of the *panzerwaffe* deep into enemy territory.' Consequently, he sent his panzer divisions off in what was to become the 'Sickle Cut' across northern France, just as he and Manstein had conceived in their hotels in Koblenz.

In a similar manner, General Hoth had been expected to consolidate his two bridgeheads into one and push the French back out of artillery range of the river and the crossing-points but, like Guderian, Rommel had other ideas! He secured the only heavy bridging available for a crossing-point that was to be shared by the panzers of both Hoth's divisions but Rommel went on to commandeer the 5th Panzer's AFVs (armoured fighting vehicles), despite General Hartlieb's protests, arguing with impeccable armoured logic that it was better to have the few panzers available at that point fighting in a single group.

7th Panzer recovery west of the Meuse. Pz IV and 38(t).

Rather than sitting tight during the 14th, Rommel ordered *Oberst* von Bismarck's 7th Rifle Regiment to advance 3 miles into enemy territory to secure the village of Onhaye, which they succeeded in doing. In breaking out of the bridgehead, the 7th Panzer had benefited from French attention being focused on counter-attacking the 5th Panzer around Haut-le-Wastia.

Poor staff work and coordination had blighted French attempts at operational level counter-attacks during 14 May but on the 15th it was organizational issues that prevented success; in this case logistical. The Char B Bis in accordance with French armoured doctrine was designed to support the infantry; consequently it had a small fuel tank and being heavy could only operate over a short range. The Chars were, however, now being used in a far more mobile role than that conceived by their designers and the distance they could travel was a problem. On the evening of the 14th the Char B Bis of the 1st French Armoured Division that were in position to crush the few German panzers across the Meuse simply didn't have the fuel and the bowsers were at the rear of the column! Rommel had been lucky. Delays the following morning and a German dive-bomber raid on the fuel column attempting to get through the traffic to the tanks only made matters worse. When Hoth's panzers attacked,

A knocked out Char 1b Bis.

the French were still in the protracted business of refuelling. The result of what would have been an unequal battle between four French tank battalions and a single weak German panzer battalion was, in the event, the destruction of the best part of the 1st French Armoured Division. During 15 May Rommel advanced a further 10 miles west to Philippeville.

That same day marked the collapse of the French on the Meuse front. The speed of the three panzer thrusts had, at Dinant, Monthermé and Sedan, coupled with the slow French reaction, precipitated a crumbling of command and control in a ponderous army that General Weygand later summed up as 'a 1918 army against a German Army of 1939. It was sheer madness.' The revolution in military affairs had taken place unnoticed under the French army's nose.

Chapter 3

Blitzkrieg

Having broken through the final line of resistance on 16 May the panzers headed north-west. They were now off the meticulously map-exercised plan that had successfully taken them through the Ardennes and across the Meuse. Later that day Guderian's XIX Panzer Corps advanced 40 miles against diminishing opposition, rounding up surprised French soldiers in the process.

Guderian passed a situation report to HQ Panzer Group Kleist by radio summarizing the day's events and confidently announced his intention to continue the pursuit on 17 May. He later wrote:

> After our splendid success on the 16th May and the simultaneous victory won by XLI Army Corps, it did not occur to me that my superiors could possibly still hold the same views as before, nor that they would now be satisfied with simply holding the bridgehead we had established across the Meuse while awaiting the arrival of the infantry corps. I was completely filled with the ideas that I had expressed during my conference with Hitler in March, that is to say to complete our break-through and not to stop until we had reached the English Channel. It certainly never occurred to me that Hitler himself, who had approved the boldest aspects of the Manstein plan and had not uttered a word against my proposals concerning exploitation of the break-through, would now be the one to be frightened by his own temerity and would order our advance to be stopped at once. Here I was making a great mistake, as I was to discover on the following morning.

Early in the morning of 17 May Guderian received a signal from Panzer Group Kleist: 'the advance was to be halted at once and I was personally to report to General von Kleist, who would come to see me at my airstrip at 0700 hours.' Von Kleist landed punctually and, without the normal pleasantries in what was their first face-to-face meeting for at least a week, ignored the startling success of his corps and berated Guderian in the strongest terms for having disobeyed orders. Guderian later wrote: 'When the first storm was passed, he had stopped to draw breath, I asked that I might be relieved of my command.' Kleist was surprised but matters between the two generals went from bad to

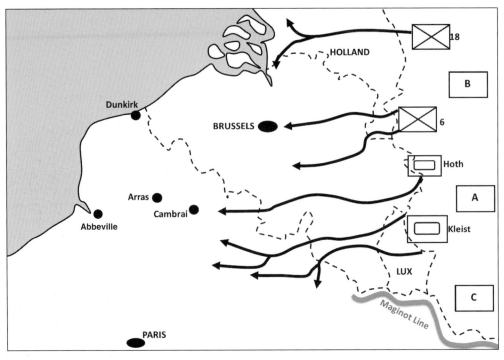

The German situation on 17 May.

worse. It eventually took the Twelfth Army's commander, General List, to pour oil on troubled waters, with a compromise that kept Guderian's HQ static but, despite *OKH* orders to halt, allowed recce in force, which the panzer commander naturally interpreted as a green light to continue!

One of the keys to German success in the 1940 campaign was communication. The importance of signals units and equipment had been learned and there was to be no repetition of the 1914 incident when the German High Command failed to realize that Liege had been captured by their own troops for three days! Radio signals emanating from the XIX Panzer Corps had been used against Guderian, whose radio nets had been monitored by the Twelfth Army and Army Group A, not only to keep abreast of the panzer spearhead's progress but also to plot the location of Corps HQ. While his divisions could move, Guderian's main headquarters could not move without being detected disobeying orders. Guderian, originally a signals officer, was, however, in this case able to avoid monitoring of his orders to stay put by his superior headquarters, simply by running out a 2.5-mile telephone cable between his main and tactical HQs!

The number of radios in both German headquarters and armoured vehicles far exceeded those in either the French or British armies of the time in not only quality but quantity as well, thanks to significant advances in German radio technology and training between 1936 and 1940. Telefunken had developed effective robust and reliable tank and recce vehicles' radios that had been the

Vehicle-mounted radios on a command vehicle during the 1940 campaign.

essence of this transformation of warfare, giving flexibility and speed of response at all levels of command across no less than 104 divisional signal battalions and twenty-three corps HQs. The proliferation of radio in the *Wehrmacht* was largely responsible for the Germans' astonishing early successes. The Allies were not able to catch up in this field until 1943.

By the evening of 17 May, the XIX Panzer Corps' spearheads had secured a crossing over the River Oise, brushing aside the 2nd French Armoured Division that was strung out along 25 miles of river line. Guderian was now some 70 miles from Sedan and far behind the Allies' northern armies. Despite the firm halt order from *OKH*, the advance continued for the next few days, with only the young Colonel de Gaulle's newly-raised 4th Armoured Division providing significant and for a time worrying opposition during 17 to 19 May.

De Gaulle's Attacks

The 4th Armoured Division was still being formed in early May 1940, with Colonel de Gaulle, an exponent of the use of armour, taking command on 11 May of the only partly-organized division. Nonetheless, de Gaulle was ordered to deploy a screen along the River Aisne around Laon but realizing the vulnerability of the panzer thrust across from his front, he decided to attack into the flank of XIX Panzer Corps near Montcornet with all his available tanks,

Charles de Gaulle.

Graf von Kielmannsegg photographed when NATO Central Army Group Commander.

three battalions of them without infantry and little other support. This also unauthorized advance took him 20 miles east of the Aisne.

The attack started well, with the French tanks brushing aside Guderian's light flank protection screen. The French were soon starting to shoot up the panzer divisions' logistic convoys but it was the 1st Panzer Division's supply officer *Oberst* Graf von Kielmannsegg who reacted to what was by now a serious and unexpected threat. Rounding up all the troops he could find including a handful of anti-tank guns and ordering his division's pioneers (engineers) to hastily lay mines, he was able to hold the French attack long enough for the convoys to be re-routed away from the area. With a handful of panzers from workshops, Kielmannsegg was eventually able to mount a counter-attack and bring the French advance to a halt. De Gaulle, being out on his own and bombed and strafed by Stukas, withdrew but his attack, according to Kielmannsegg, was the only French counter-attack that was 'completely correct in terms of time, place and direction'.

De Gaulle tried again two days later but this time the Germans were alert to his division's presence and quickly blocked the attack.

Final Dash to the Channel

Meanwhile, on the evening of 17 May the restrictions on headlong advance, which most of the panzer commanders had circumvented in various ways, were lifted and the final dash to the Channel was on. The 2nd Panzer Division covered 55 miles in a single day crossing the First World War Somme battlefields, in the process destroying the widely-dispersed brigades of the 12th (Eastern) Division, one of the three low establishment Territorial Army divisions sent to join the BEF for entrenching duties. This division had, for example, just four Mk I 25-pounders rather than the established seventy-two! Their presence and determination slowed the Germans by a matter of hours but at 0200 hours on 21 May the 2nd Rifle Regiment reached the Channel coast. The 6th and 8th Panzer divisions would reach the coast early the following morning. It had taken just under ten days for *Panzergruppe* Kleist to cut off the Allied northern group of armies!

18–25 pounder and limber.

The 7th Panzer Division

Meanwhile, Rommel's advance had, if anything, been even more successful (described as 'impetuous' or less critically 'audacious' by some German historians), certainly in its early stages, but by 16 May the Allies had realized the error of the Dyle Plan that saw them advance 70 miles into Belgium, deep into the German *Fall Gelb* envelopment. Hitler is said to have remarked: 'I could have wept for joy; they had fallen into the trap.' Consequently, the northern panzer thrusts were halted, in the case of the 7th Panzer Division, on the evening of 17 May around Cambrai, as elements of the First French Army turned south to meet the threat to their rear. Rommel had driven 50 miles deep into the French rear area that day, spreading confusion and completing the overthrow of another French armoured formation. Nonetheless, Hoth's corps was to await the arrival of the infantry, while his panzer divisions – now critically short of combat supplies – rested, reorganized and replenished.

This completed, despite Hoth's concern that his soldiers were exhausted, on the afternoon of 19 May Rommel argued that a resumption of the advance after over twenty-four hours stationary and a good moonlit night in prospect would yield results and cost fewer casualties.

A book recently published in Germany attributes the early German military successes to widespread use of the drug Pervitin to keep the panzer crews awake and alert. While this is an exaggeration, it certainly helps to account for the remarkable endurance of the panzers. The use of this drug has been confirmed and was the brand name of a performance-enhancing drug having the same chemical constituents as crystal meth!

At 0140 hours on 20 May Rommel, mounted in his armoured command post vehicle, resumed his 'impetuous' advance, this time directed on Arras, with his two panzer battalions leading. He was not going to be able to make such progress as he had during the period 14 to 16 May, but that is to anticipate events (see below).

Redeploying French divisions from the First Army made themselves felt during the course of the day but not as General Billotte, commander of the northern First Army Group, had intended. He had ordered a coordinated counterstroke by three armoured divisions but all that materialized were small forces inserting themselves across the line of 7th Panzer Division's march to Arras. The Germans, however, had become strung out.

Rommel holding an O (Orders) Group with his senior commanders during the 1940 campaign, looking at the air action above.

Rommel at the front supervising the crossing of an overbridged demolition.

The essence of the problem was that the 38(t) tanks that made up the bulk of the 7th Panzer Division's tank fleet had made good progress since 0140 hours and by 0600 had reached Beaurains, a couple of miles short of Arras, with, as normal, the divisional commander up at the front. The four panzer grenadier battalions mounted in trucks were, however, all lagging behind. Consequently, French forces probing forward from the line of the Canal du Nord and the River Sensée infiltrated into the gap between the panzers and the panzer grenadiers and Rommel returning back towards Cambrai in an armoured car, escorted by a single tank, to inject urgency into the infantry, had to run the gauntlet of French infantry and some light armour. The escorting tank was knocked out and for several hours Rommel was pinned down in the gap and only eventually released by his advancing panzer grenadiers.

SS Obergruppenführer Theodor Eicke, commander of the Totenkopf Division.

The 7th Panzer Division spent the rest of 20 May probing the defences of Arras but the division had come up against the British Petreforce and elements of the 23rd Division.

What is less well-known, largely through the long-standing *Wehrmacht* dislike of the fully-motorized *SS Totenkopf* Division (*SSTK*), is that elements of this division had been rushed forward from reserve, way back on the Meuse at Dinant, to intervene to extricate Rommel from a situation of his own making.

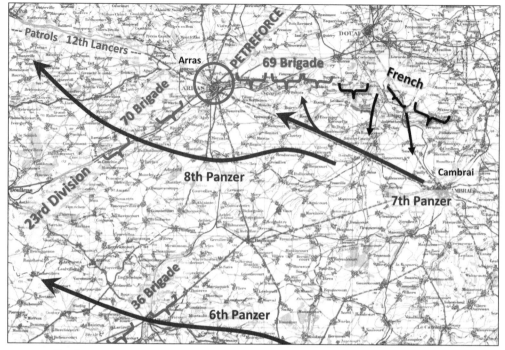

Cambrai – Arras, 20 May 1940.

The *Totenkopf* spent the day fighting a savage action to clear French colonial troops from villages on Rommel's open right flank and eventually took 1,600 prisoners, mainly Moroccans. Later in the day the *SSTK* beat off a belated French armoured attack that would otherwise again have cut through the 7th Panzer Division's line of advance between Cambrai and Arras on the evening of 20 May.

SS Totenkopf *badge.*

Arras, 20 May 1940

The Allies, as we will see, had identified the city of Arras as being a vital road communications node on the southern flank of the Northern Group of Armies and had established Petreforce in the city; an ad hoc force of GHQ defence troops and logistic units. To either flank the two brigades of the 23rd (Northumbrian) Division,[1] also a low establishment 'entrenching division', were deployed with 69 Brigade in positions on the River Scarpe to the east, linking up with the French, while 70 Brigade was caught taking up positions to the south of the city by the 8th Panzer Division and all but destroyed as it passed

---

1. This was a second line division, not to be confused with the 50th (Northumbrian) Division.

Officers of the 23rd Division at an Orders Group.

Arras. The brigade included the 10th and 11th battalions of the Durham Light Infantry, who were attacked on the very ground that their sister battalions would cover on the following day in the 'Arras counter-attack'. 8th Panzer Division continued its dash and, as already noted, was only 15 miles from the coast by nightfall, being behind and to the right of the 2nd Panzer Division.

12th Lancers' badge.

The move of the 8th Panzer around Arras had not, however, been uneventful, their tail tangling with the British 12th Lancers whose three armoured car squadrons were tasked to recce the area around Arras, as far as Bapaume, Péronne, Amiens and Doullens. As far as the British were concerned, the situation south of Arras was far from clear, with rumours abounding regarding the German penetration of the French lines. During the withdrawal from the Dyle, the Lancers had been used in a role more suitable for the light tanks but this reconnaissance task was a job for which they were trained and equipped: find the enemy, determine his intentions and report.

Before the Lancers could go into action they had to complete a 30-mile drive south to the Arras area. Consequently, by the time the regiment arrived the Germans were well into their day's operations. The Lancers' intent was for the

A patrol of C Squadron, 12th Lancers mounted in a Morris model CS9 armoured car armed with a Boys anti-tank rifle and a Bren gun.

squadrons to fan out across the Somme: A Squadron was deployed to the right and was to probe towards Amiens; B Squadron, in the centre, was to head south towards Bapaume and Péronne; and C Squadron was sent out to the left in the direction of Cambrai. In the event none of the squadrons got anywhere near these objectives, which is an indication of how little the British knew from the French of the enemy's progress. The armoured cars of B and C squadrons had only travelled a very short distance when they encountered the enemy, south and east of the city, reporting that they 'ran into numerous panzers' who were almost certainly Rommel's tank regiment. A Squadron made better progress and reached Avesnes, some 10 miles west, before they found the enemy. Here they had a sharp engagement with elements of the 8th Panzer Division. One of the squadron's patrols, however, shadowed a German armoured unit heading towards St. Pol, again almost certainly the 8th Panzer. As dusk fell, the regiment leaguered north of Festubert and spent the night there servicing their vehicles and getting such rest as they could.

Chapter 4

The British Expeditionary Force

Work on producing a so-called New British Expeditionary Force had begun in 1936, but with the spectre of the First World War and a slow recovery from the Great Depression Britain was reluctant to re-arm. This was despite the fact that 'the bomber will always get through' doctrine had, by the late 1930s, firmly placed the front-line defence of Britain not on the Channel coast but well into northern France, Belgium and Holland. This unpleasant fact was well-known to politicians but repeatedly ignored.

The reality of a resurgent Germany, however, meant that the first tentative steps were made to re-arm but it took the Munich Crisis of 1938 for concrete action to be taken. Registration for conscription and a proper re-armament programme got under way. Tentative talks with the French began over the deployment of the 'New BEF' to France in the event of renewed war with Germany.

In early 1939 authority was finally given for the Territorial Force (TF) to be 'doubled'. For example, the 6th Battalion, Durham Light Infantry (6 DLI) had their part of the county split in two, with the new 10th Battalion taking half and recruiting being stepped up, aiming to produce a pair of fully-manned battalions within a year. A broadly similar measure to increase the number of units had been seen in September 1914, but in the case of the Second World War, Territorial battalions were only brought up to strength with conscripts once war was declared.

With the doubling of the Territorials, the number of TF divisions was increased from thirteen to twenty-six. Two of these divisions, the 12th and 23rd, rushed out to France as has been mentioned in the previous chapters, feature peripherally in the story of Arras 'Counter-Attack' 1940.

In February 1939, having previously been Assistant Director of Mechanisation in the War Office, the by now Major General Martel took command of the 50th Northumbrian Infantry Division (TF) to oversee the doubling of the Territorial Force. Martel's division was also in the process of becoming fully motorized, i.e. using trucks and other vehicles in lieu of horse-drawn wagons, etc. The 50th Division now consisted of two brigades, 150 and 151. It was the latter Brigade who were to take part in the 'Arras counter-attack' in May 1940.

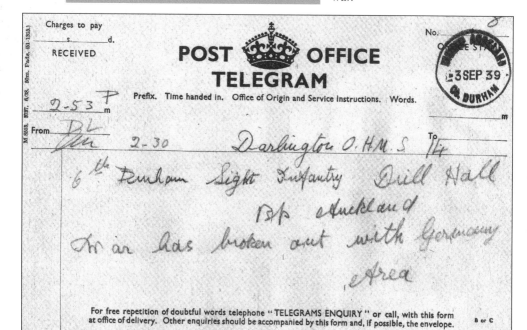

TERRITORIAL ARMY

VACANCIES

for suitable YOUNG MEN of 17 years of age and over in the

6th Battalion

THE DURHAM LIGHT INFANTRY

A FORTNIGHT'S ANNUAL CAMP WITH PAY

including marriage allowance for men of 21 years of age and over

Uniform provided.   Sports.   Recreation Room.

ANNUAL PROFICIENCY GRANT
£3 10s.—RISING TO £5.

Travelling Expenses paid for attendance at Drills.

FOR FULL PARTICULARS APPLY AT THE

DRILL HALL, UNION STREET, BISHOP AUCKLAND.

A pre-war recruiting poster after the doubling of the Territorials.

Telegram: outbreak of war.

Charges to pay s. d. RECEIVED

POST OFFICE TELEGRAM

Prefix. Time handed in. Office of Origin and Service Instructions. Words.

No.

3 SEP 39

2-53 P.m

From 2-30 Darlington O.H.M.S

6th Durham Light Infantry Drill Hall Bishop Auckland War has broken out with Germany Area

For free repetition of doubtful words telephone " TELEGRAMS ENQUIRY " or call, with this form at office of delivery. Other enquiries should be accompanied by this form and, if possible, the envelope.   B or C

Troops of the 'New BEF' embark and arrive in France.

On the outbreak of war on 4 September 1939, the first wave of four Regular Army divisions was deployed to France, forming two corps positioned on the borders of neutral Belgium by 11 October. They were followed during the eight months of the Phoney War by the 5th Division before the end of the year and the BEF was subsequently joined by three TF divisions, including the 50th, during January and February. They were followed by two more immediately before the German attack on the West. In addition, there were the three low establishment entrenching divisions – the 12th, 23rd and 46th – who arrived in France during April. By the time of the German attack on the West in May 1940 the BEF, initially 158,000-strong, had expanded to three corps of 316,000 men.

The first task of the BEF in France was to take over the construction of border fortifications that had been begun by the French, digging defensive positions and long lengths of anti-tank ditch and working on wiring and mining strongpoints normally based on French-built 1937-vintage concrete pillboxes. By early spring 1940 III Corps had taken control of most of the Territorial divisions and was overseeing and attempting to balance the conflicting demands of training and, as we will see from the 50th Division's experience, labouring

The BEF in France during the Phoney War.

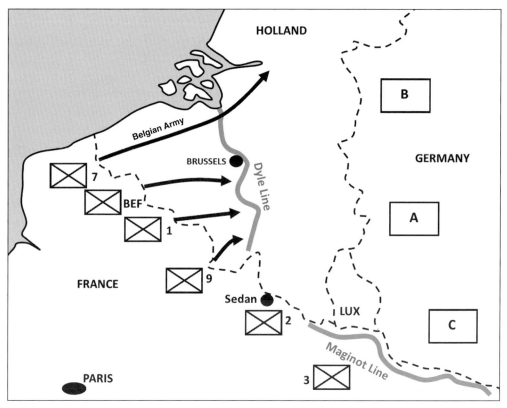

The Dyle Plan.

on defences as well. All this First World War-style digging during the Phoney War seriously distracted the BEF from proper military training and preparations for the campaign.

An irony is that with the French commander-in-chief's Dyle Plan, known somewhat transparently as Plan D, these fortifications would be abandoned once Belgium was invaded and the Allies invited into their country by the Belgian government. The BEF, along with the First, Seventh and Ninth French armies making up the French First Army Group, were to advance rapidly some 60 miles to the line Antwerp, River Dyle, Gembloux Gap and the Belgian section of the River Meuse. No reconnaissance of neutral Belgium would, of course, be possible and the whole plan, which would take several days to implement, was dependent on the Belgian army holding its forward defences on the Albert Canal long enough for deployment to take place.

The BEF's Armour
The BEF was fully mechanized but in the rush to expand and prepare defences, it was mostly only partly trained by the time of the invasion. One of its key weaknesses was that it only had a single tank brigade plus two light armoured

Mark VIB Light Tank.

Cruiser MK I tanks of the 1st Armoured Division training in the UK.

brigades equipped with the light tank, suitable only for reconnaissance.

Even though the Germans had placed their panzer divisions at the heart of *Fall Gelb*, the British armoured component was minimal, the light reconnaissance brigades (one Territorial) were equipped with light tanks and 1 Army Tank Brigade with Mk I and II (Matilda) infantry tanks. In addition, there were four cavalry regiments, including the 12th Lancers, equipped with armoured cars, also in the reconnaissance role.

The British were forming the 1st Armoured Division in the UK from the 'Mobile Division' originally raised in October 1937. It was to be developed into a tank-heavy formation designed for rapid mobile operations, exploitation and reconnaissance in force. However, only once the invasion of the West had begun and the fighting was well under way did the division deploy to France. They arrived as the crisis was deepening and the opportunity to use the division's armoured mobility and punch had already passed. Fighting with little support and a fragmentary deployment including the defence of Calais under hastily-arranged command structures, the division could not show its potential.

The 50th Northumbrian Division
In some appalling winter weather at the end of January 1945, General Martel was ordered to deploy his division from their billets in Oxfordshire via Southampton and Cherbourg and on to a concentration area near Le Mans. After many difficulties the division arrived at its allocated training area west of Amiens on 28 February, where they were billeted in houses, factories and farms. Here serious motorized training got under way, particularly the art of quickly embussing and debussing from the platoon of Royal Army Service Corps trucks that each battalion now had under its command. A series of increasingly exacting brigade and divisional exercises followed.

After a month's training including some live firing, in early April the division moved to the area south of Lille where they took over labouring duties, i.e. digging. They worked in shifts on defences of II Corps' reserve line, the key feature of which was a 20ft wide and 8ft deep anti-tank ditch. The divisional historian recorded that even though the many miners in the ranks of the division had not been at the coalface for eight months, their digging and revetting skills were second to none. Consequently, all requests for mechanical assistance were turned down on the basis that the Northumbrian Division's battalions were digging faster than those who already had mechanical diggers.

It was while still carrying out these labouring tasks that the 50th Division received the code word BIRCH at 0700 hours on 10 May 1940. The German invasion of the West had begun.

III Corps, who commanded the Territorial Force divisions, remained in reserve with some elements of the 50th Division; for example, assisting with traffic and refugee control. The remainder continued digging, live firing and training, despite many spy and fifth column scares.

Invasion and Plan D

Army Group A advanced through the Ardennes, spearheaded by Guderian's XIX Panzer Corps amid a news blackout, while the attack on Belgium and Holland with *fallschirmjäger* and the northern panzer thrusts received much press coverage, as did Army Group C's fixing attack on the Maginot Line. This, combined with the preconceived notion that the Ardennes were impenetrable and the complex and ponderous French command system, meant it was belatedly realized that the aim of the *Fall Gelb* plan was to envelop the Allied northern armies. Army Group B's attack had successfully drawn the Allies deeper into the unfolding envelopment. A ghastly mistake!

See maps on page 19 and 51.

On reaching the River Dyle, the BEF had deployed to the north of the French First Army. I Corps was on the right flank, with the 2nd Division on the right and 1st Division on the left. The 48th Infantry Division TF was the Corps' reserve. The left or northern flank was held by II Corps, with only the 3rd Division deployed forward and the 4th Division in reserve. The Belgian army held the sector on the BEF's left flank, north to the sea.

Initially, Army Group B's blows in Belgium fell most heavily on the First French Army, with Major General Bernard Montgomery's 3rd Division being the only element of the BEF to heavily engage with the enemy, in its case east of Louvain, on 14 May.

On the following day, a German attack developed along virtually the whole

British troops passing through Louvain in Mk I scout carriers.

line held by the BEF. Two German corps attacked: IV Corps mounted assaults on the positions held by the 2nd Division, with XI Corps continuing to attack those held by the 3rd Division. These German corps only made limited gains against the British defences on the left flank.

On the BEF's right flank the Germans penetrated 3 miles into the 2nd Division's positions. Consequently, Lord Gort withdrew I Corps to form a coherent defensive line some miles to the rear. However, with the realization of the threat that was developing from the Ardennes, this was only the first step in what would be a further three stages of withdrawal over the three nights, to the line of the River Escaut, between 16 and 19 May.

Use of Armour
Shortly after the German invasion of Belgium, Brigadier Vyvyan Pope, who had relinquished command of the 3rd Armoured Brigade in East Anglia, arrived at Gort's headquarters to take up the post of GHQ Armoured Advisor to the BEF. Not having been aware of Plan D, he was appalled at the prospect of sending 1 Army Tank Brigade forward on its tracks and the fact that officers right up the chain of command

> had not bothered to acquaint themselves with the capabilities and limitations of armour. I am not at all happy about the move of 1 Army Tank Brigade… They can scarcely realise that A11s and A12s [Mk I and Mk II (Matilda)] are not designed for and are not mechanically capable of long marches on their tracks.

His advice came too late, the plan was set in stone and the brigade moved forward on its tracks, there being no tank transporters. In the event, 1 Army Tank Brigade did not see action in this first phase of the campaign, remaining

Matilda Mark II tank.

in reserve behind I and II Corps.

The 50th (Northumbrian) Division

Rumours were rife in the rear areas and on 15 May the expected orders were received by the 50th Division to motor through the stream of refugees forward to the Dendre Canal where they were to prepare defences to facilitate the withdrawal of I and II Corps from the Dyle Line. The battalions dug defensive positions, which they were to hold long enough for forward divisions to withdraw through them and for the bridges, locks and weirs to be blown. The 50th Division was then to retire behind the next main defensive line on the Escaut Canal.

As it transpired, at 0600 hours on 18 May the division began its move back without having come into contact with German ground troops and had only been lightly attacked by the *Luftwaffe*. No transport was available and no clear destination given, so the theoretically-motorized 50th Division began a two-day westward march of over 50 miles in increasingly hot conditions to an unknown future. As they marched they had to contend with what was now a flood of Belgian refugees anxious to avoid a repetition of the terrible 1914–18 German occupation of their country, which all too many of them recalled from twenty-two years earlier.

It was a tired and footsore division that reached Lannoy, 5 miles east of Lille, at 2000 hours on 19 May. Their halt here was, however, brief as the 50th Division had a new task and RASC trucks were on their way to pick them up and take them another 25 miles further south to La Bassée where they arrived

Refugees made movement by road a slow process.

at 0330 hours the following morning. Here they were to take up defensive positions on the infamous La Bassée Canal facing south rather than east, as during the First World War. Something was clearly wrong! According to the DLI historian 'the divisional rumour mill soon confirmed that it was very wrong!'

Counter-Attack Plans

During 19 May General Pownall, Lord Gort's chief of staff, telephoned the War Office and for the first time raised the possibility of withdrawal. This and other conversations that day were almost certainly monitored by the French and set events in train in London.

Churchill and the War Cabinet were dismayed that a withdrawal to the coast and evacuation were even being considered by Gort. General Ironside, Chief of Imperial Staff (CIGS), was instructed to fly to France that night and order the BEF to move south-west and force their way through the German panzer corridor in order to join the French armies that were still fighting to the south. General Dill, as Vice CIGS, was to reinforce this in person in a visit to General Georges, commander of the forces in the north east.

The politicians' instructions were unrealistic and by the time they were issued,

Lord Gort and Lieutenant General Pownall.

impossible to execute. Five of Gort's battle-worthy divisions were in contact with the enemy and even if they could have broken contact, a gap would be left that the Germans could exploit and the Belgians would be isolated. Not only that, GHQ staff reported that they had only four days' combat supplies and sufficient ammunition for only one battle was available. Somewhat reluctantly, Lord Gort agreed that he would with two divisions attack to meet a significant French counter-attack from the south on 21 May. Events were now under way that would lead to the 'Arras counter-attack'.

General Ironside.

General Dill travelled to General Billotte's headquarters near Lens, where he found the commander of First Army Group 'in a state of complete depression'. Grabbing him, the angry Ironside shook the French general by the buttons of his tunic. That evening the British generals returned to the UK and Ironside confided to his diary: 'God help the BEF, brought to this state by the incompetence of the French Command.'

Eventually General Billotte ordered General Prioux's Cavalry Corps of two light mechanized divisions to attack south to the Somme on 19 May but having lost heavily in the Battle of the Gembloux Gap, it was greatly weakened and more than a little demoralized. Lord Gort was to attack towards Cambrai and the Somme with the BEF. There was, however, to be no counter-attack from the south on 21 May, the reason being that by this point in the campaign the French command and control system was becoming paralysed by the speed of German movement. With their linear minds locked in the practices of the previous war, few senior French officers could cope with enemy breakthrough and penetration. With headquarters being overrun or forced to move, the passage of information and orders became increasingly difficult. The multiplicity of levels of command, often with the added hindrance of overlapping responsibilities, the French system was slow and unresponsive. By the time information had been gathered, digested and orders issued (and reached those concerned), the situation had invariably changed on the ground, making most edicts from the chain of command irrelevant and confusing. In modern parlance, the Germans were operating within the French decision-making cycle.

In addition, General Weygand, who took over from Gamelin as the French commander-in-chief during 19 May, promptly cancelled the partly-formed French counter-attack plans and went to bed. All of this was, of course, going to have a severe impact on the conduct of Lord Gort's 'counter-attack' south towards the Somme.

Chapter 5

Concentration and Orders

With Lord Gort having assured Ironside that he would attack south to help the French cut the panzer corridor, the 5th and 50th divisions were set in motion towards Arras. His aim was to incorporate these two divisions, plus 1 Army Tank Brigade and the 12th Lancers who would be the reconnaissance element, in a force under the senior divisional commander, Major General Franklyn (5th Division). Frankforce was its name and it would concentrate around Vimy Ridge, north of Arras.

The essence of the orders Generals Franklyn and Martel (50th Division) received from the commander-in-chief on the evening of 19 May was that they were to improve the position around Arras by driving the Germans away from the city; a much-reduced aim and not at all the counterstroke that Ironside had ordered Lord Gort to undertake earlier in the day. The situation had, however, changed in as much as the BEF's commander was aware that Weygand had cancelled or at least postponed the French counter-attack from the south. If it was to be a part of the Allied counterstroke, British operations around Arras would only be a preliminary phase.

General Franklyn, 5th Division.

The verbal orders that General Franklyn recalled receiving from Lord Gort began with a preamble about cutting off the German panzers' line of communication, but the specific instructions were as follows:

1. To move to Arras, dealing with any enemy, which we might or might not meet en route.
2. To relieve French armoured troops holding the line of the River Scarpe, east of Arras, and also any British, which I might find there.
3. To make Arras secure, gaining as much elbow room as possible south of the town.
4. To the best of my memory, Gort used the term 'mopping up'. I certainly got the impression that I was only likely to encounter weak German detachments.

The troops already in place around Arras were Petreforce, an ad hoc body of GHQ units based on the largely ineffective remains of the 12th Division. The only significant units in Arras were the 1st Battalion, Welsh Guard and Cook's Light Horse and an ad hoc squadron-sized sub-unit made up of a variety of tanks that had been in workshops there. As has already been mentioned, the under-resourced and under-trained 23rd Division had 69 Brigade north-east of the city dug in on the line of the River Scarpe and 70 Brigade was the formation caught to the west of Arras by the 8th Panzer Division before it could properly deploy and was virtually destroyed. As a result, the barely-trained 69 Brigade was to be withdrawn as soon as possible and replaced by elements of Frankforce from the 5th Division.

The first elements of Frankforce in action on 20 May, as already mentioned, were the 12th Lancers whose three armoured car squadrons were tasked to recce the area around Arras, as far as Bapaume, Péronne, Amiens and Doullens. The situation south of Arras was far from clear, with rumours abounding regarding the German penetration of the French lines.

Morris CS9/Light Armoured Car as used by 12th Lancers.

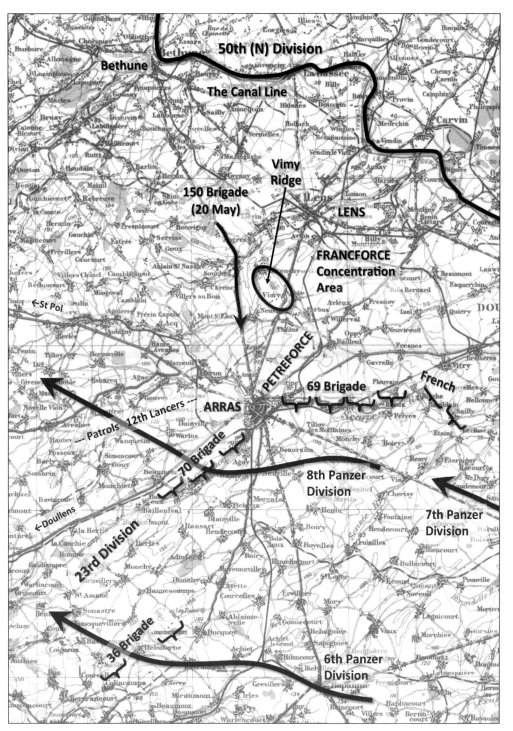

The situation on 20 May, as assumed by the British.

The 12th Lancers were in action south of Arras on the afternoon of 20 May; however, they were not the only reconnaissance force deployed that afternoon. The light tanks of the recce troop, the 4 RTR, were also deployed to cover the move of 1 Army Tank Brigade into Vimy. Well to the south-west atop a ridge near St. Amand they saw a German panzer column advancing north-west, which that far west could have been either from the 6th or 8th Panzer division. Following a brief exchange of fire, the German advance guard deployed to attack and, wisely, pausing only to send a contact report by Morse code, the recce troop withdrew to join the rest of the regiment that was supposed to have been arriving at Vimy.

Meanwhile, General Martel had left Headquarters 50th Division north of the La Bassée Canal at dawn, moving ahead of 150 Brigade to Arras. His first stop was at HQ Petreforce and he was not impressed with the state of the defences of the thinly-spread Welsh Guards, who were exhausted and had very few anti-tank guns available. It was clear that his first task was to secure Arras, let alone the surrounding area. Consequently, General Martel detached a battalion of 150 Brigade to Petreforce, plus an anti-tank battery and a company of Royal Engineers.

During a visit to the Regimental HQ of the 12th Lancers, General Martel learned of the wider situation, in particular the move of German armour on the roads west to Doullens and St. Pol. Of the French, however, the Lancers had little information, other than that the 3rd Light Mechanised Division (3rd DLM, *3rd Division Légère Mécanisée*) was strung out along the line of the Scarpe. These French troops, mainly Somua tanks, crop up along the river line and around Arras throughout the story of the 'counter-attack'.

Major General Franklyn arrived later in the afternoon and planning began in earnest. He made some immediate adjustments: the remainder of 150 Brigade would take up positions in Arras, while 13 Brigade – the first brigade of the 5th Division to arrive – would relieve elements of the 3rd DLM on the Scarpe east of the city during the night. This latter measure would free up that division with some seventy Somua S35 tanks to concentrate to the north-west of Arras in order to take part in operations the following day. It was originally intended that 150 Brigade would carry out the offensive part of the coming operation but that task now fell to 151 Brigade.

The latter had begun the day at dawn with battalion recces of defensive positions on the Canal Line but at 0515 hours these orders were cancelled and they received a warning order for another move south to hold the Vimy area just north of Arras. 25 Brigade, one of the fragile Territorial brigades attached to the 50th Division, would follow south to the concentration area when transport was available.

The history of the 6th DLI relates events of the move that can be generalized to the rest of the brigade and illustrates the increasing dislocation, not only of the French, but of the BEF as well:

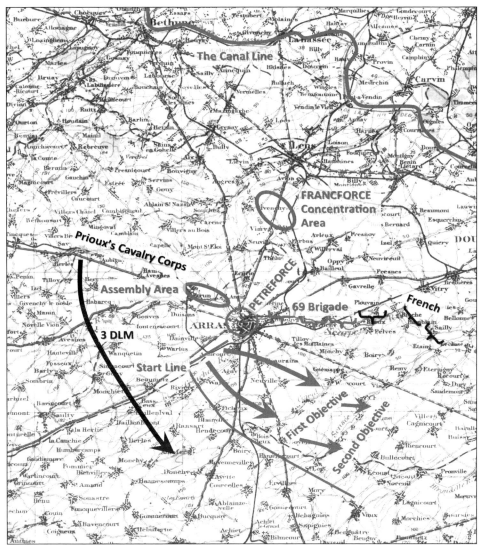

Outline of the Frankforce Plan.

This move was to be made by trucks. Second-Lieutenant TA Cookson and four men went to Neuve-Chapelle to collect the transport. There was none to be had, though a promise was made that it would be sent on to the Battalion as soon as it arrived at Brigade. In view of the increasingly critical position at Arras, it was decided at 11.05 a.m., to send an advanced group up to Vimy Ridge to reconnoitre and hold positions which the Battalion would move to when transport arrived to carry them. 'D' Company and the Carrier Platoon, under Major Jeffreys, reached Thélus on the Ridge at about noon. 'D' Company took up position between the Lens-Arras road and the Thélus-Roclincourt road, with the

BEF transport being used for carrying troops.

carriers patrolling between the right of the company and Neuville-St-Vaast. Major Jeffreys with one of the carriers conducted a reconnaissance.

Other than the attentions of the *Luftwaffe* several days earlier, this was the closest the battalion had come to action. With clouds of smoke coming from Arras and the sound of shellfire clearly audible, D Company needed little encouragement to dig in, despite the heat of the afternoon. Coincidentally this was on the same battlefield where, twenty-odd years earlier, their forebears had entrenched. Indeed, rusting First World War barbed wire and pickets were collected and strung around the company's position.

The advance groups were joined at 1400 hours by a company from the 4th Royal Northumberland Fusiliers (4 RNF), 50th Division's Motor Cycle Battalion, who with their motor cycles and sidecars plus a pair of armoured cars patrolled forward of the defensive position.

All, however, was not well back at the Canal Line; the rest of the brigade, after concentrating around Hulloch, sat and waited for their transport. Also – in their case vainly – waiting for RASC trucks was 25 Brigade. It was only at 2200 hours that transport eventually arrived, finally delivering the exhausted 151 Brigade to the Vimy area at 0330 hours on 21 May. Even though it was now apparent that 151 Brigade would be conducting the offensive part of the operation, so tired were the men that General Martel gave strict instructions that the orders process was not to begin until the following morning; all ranks were to rest.

Meanwhile, the Territorial Force 92nd Field Regiment Royal Artillery (two batteries each of twelve Mk I 25-pounders) had moved south to Arras and had been ordered to be regrouped from the 5th

4th RNF motor cycles.

Division to the 50th Northumberland, the latter not having artillery in its order of battle at this stage in the war. An excellent and revealing account of the

18-pounder Mk IV or Carriage Mk IV. A transitional gun.

Mark II 25-pounder – not used in France 1940 but very much a part of the sequence of development.

RA Badge.

gunners' part in the following day's operations was written by 'Gun Buster' after the campaign and will be quoted from at some length. Writing under a pseudonym due to wartime security regulations, Captain Richard Austin, Battery Captain (second-in-command) of 368 Field Battery, referred to his regiment as '2004 Regiment' and the batteries 'X' and 'Y'.

92nd Field Regiment had been in action covering the 5th Division's withdrawal from the Dyle position but had pulled back to Neuve Chapelle. 'Gun Buster' wrote:

We had just finished breakfast when the Major hurried into the mess. 'Be ready to move in half an hour,' he said. 'We're going on to Vimy. We may be in action there.' Once more the guns were hooked in, and once more we took the road, through Lens, murky and depressing despite the bright day, and south towards Vimy. Now we got caught in a new flood of refugees, French this time, fleeing north from Arras and the surrounding districts with the one hope of getting to the Channel ports. The same heartrending procession, on wheels and on foot. Thousands and thousands and thousands of refugees, all pressing in one direction, driven on by ceaseless terror, without order and without control. And struggling to force a passage in the opposite direction through this panic-stricken army were all the machines of war, British and French, tanks, guns, mortars, companies of mitrailleuses with motor cycles, their heavy machine-guns carried in side-cars, and trucks upon trucks of infantry. The confusion and shouting and screaming and cursing was a war in itself. Often a farm-cart would decide to pull out and try to pass the vehicle in front. Then the entire military column was held up till the chaos died down a bit. That sometimes took half an hour. This in a speed-war when every minute was precious, and an obstreperous farm-cart might lose us a lump of France!

It took 368 Battery over five hours to cover just 20 miles to Vimy and, with 70 Brigade being destroyed during the passage of the 8th Panzer Division around the south and west of Arras, they were promptly ordered to deploy for action to the east of Vimy Ridge. 'Gun Buster' was directed up onto the ridge itself with the battery observation post (OP):

It was nearly four in the afternoon when I put my head over the top of Vimy Ridge for the first time, and gazed on the battle in the distance. To the left lay Arras, in the middle distance of the plain, but a thick curtain of smoke hung before it. A bombing attack was in progress, and the heavy explosions punctuated the continual distant thunder of the gun-fire. Now and again the sound of sharp vicious bursts of machine-gun fire mingled with the heavier boom. Beyond this incessant rumble of storm, no sign of war marred the level landscape that stretched far away to Mont St. Eloi.

With the help of my OP Ack [bombardier assistant], my telephone operator, and one spade, I excavated a hole on the Lens side of the ridge in which I could stand and observe, only my head projecting over the top. A couple of wires were laid to the guns in case one was broken by enemy shell-fire. At any moment now orders to shell the enemy might be expected. But the hours went by and they never came. Yonder at Arras the Welsh Guards, with a rock-like defence, were stemming, for the time being, the central advance.

Night fell, and on the screen of darkness along the horizon the battle became more visible. The whole front lit up with red flashes of bursting bombs and shells. Two big fires were blazing and the glare coloured the sky a dirty pink. One bomb had evidently found a petrol store, and the flames were ascending in great rolling billows. High in the sky, above all this, an incredible firework display went on for hours. Tracer shells made weird and wonderful designs in fiery orange loops. Now and again up shot a rocket which burst into a ball of brilliant coloured light that shone for a few seconds and vanished. Less frequently, Very Lights burst, either red, green, blue or yellow, which floated about for a full half-minute before expiring. As a spectacle it was tremendous.

Earlier in the day another part of the assembling force was under orders to head for the Frankforce concentration area around Vimy. Brigadier Pope arrived at Orchies, some 35 miles north of Arras, with orders for 1 Army Tank Brigade to regroup with Frankforce. Their commander, Brigadier Pratt went on ahead to join the other commanders of Frankforce, leaving the 4th and 7th battalions, Royal Tank Regiment (4 and 7 RTR) to follow. Vyvyan Pope wrote:

> In the late afternoon I went down the Lens-Arras road to see the Brigade into harbour on Vimy Ridge. The move was being watched by a German Reconnaissance plane, so I halted the front of the column near Avion, just south of Lens, and told them not to move on till dusk to Vimy. I then went in search of Pratt and/or General Martel. I was told

Brigadier Vyvyan Pope, Armoured Advisor HQ BEF.

> they were on Vimy Ridge, so I went up there. The place was littered with transport and troops, but a prolonged search failed to find either commander. As I had made up my mind to come away, three Messerschmitts came over flying very low and began to machine-gun the ridge and the troops indiscriminately.

As a result of a halt to avoid the *Luftwaffe* until dusk, approximately 2100 hours, with the other military traffic crowding onto the roads at that time plus the refugees, the brigade's tanks only dribbled into the assembly area. Even though they had not been in action, it had by the night of 20 May lost over 25 per cent of its tanks, largely due to approximately 150 miles of motoring on their tracks. This move, as with those of the 5th and 50th divisions, was conducted in radio silence.

Ju 87 Stuka diver bombers in action over France.

Second Lieutenant Vaux, the recce troop commander, arrived at Petit Vimy and reported to Regimental Headquarters (RHQ) of 4 RTR late at night. His commanding officer, Lieutenant Colonel Fitzmaurice, was aware that enemy tanks were approaching Arras. 'I shall have work for you tomorrow, so get some food and into that bed at once.' Knowing that there was only one bed in the cottage, Vaux protested that the CO should have it, but he replied: 'You are worn out; do what you are told.' Colonel Fitzmaurice then got his blankets and went to sleep on the floor; it was his last night on this earth.

Meanwhile, Brigadier Pope eventually met up with General Franklyn who was clearly not expecting any action until 22 May. Pope, having come from GHQ, disabused Franklyn, telling him that 'the C-in-C expected an attack on the morrow.' Therefore, late in the evening General Franklyn had a conference in his HQ at Vimy but little could be decided because he had no idea when troops to carry out the attack would arrive and anyway the situation was likely to have changed once more. One thing, however, was already plain: 25 Brigade was too far away to make a timely arrival and with 150 and 13 brigades already taking up positions in Arras and on the Scarpe, the offensive element of the plan would inevitably fall to Brigadier Jackie Churchill's 151 Brigade. General Martel would be in overall charge of the operation.

When Brigadier Pope returned to GHQ he reported to the deputy chief of staff, General Leese, who was horrified at the idea of delay and 'after discussion with the French, who showed little signs of wishing to accelerate matters, and with Franklyn on the telephone, decided to attend a special conference at Franklyn's HQ at 6 am, 21 May.'

Pope and Leese met Franklyn at 0515 where it was agreed that the attack should begin at 1400 hours but to get to the start line – the Arras-Doullens road – the tanks, and more to the point the infantry, would have to march the best part of 8 miles from Vimy Ridge.

To meet this deadline, General Franklyn immediately summoned his Orders Group (O Gp) to assemble in Vimy at 0600 hours where he outlined his plan. *See map on page 63.* In Phase One, 151 Brigade and 1 Army Tank Brigade were to take a westerly loop around Arras and clear the area south of Arras, with the French 3rd DLM, it was promised, covering their right flank. In Phase Two, 13 Brigade was to advance south from its present defensive positions across the River Scarpe. This, depending on one's interpretation of the aim, would either tactically create a defensive position of two infantry brigades supported by tanks 4 miles south of Arras, or operationally provide a firm base for the rest of Frankforce to mount its part in the Allied counterstroke to cut the panzer corridor.

It was expected, at least by GHQ, that with the arrival of the whole of Frankforce the operation could be extended further south down to Cambrai and Bapaume on 22 May in order to meet up with a French thrust from south to north.

General Martel then made his plan for a hook around Arras to the west, based on intelligence that enemy tanks were south and south-west of Arras 'in numbers believed not to be great'. He later wrote: 'The operation resolved itself into clearing an area about ten miles deep and four miles wide, and I stated that I propose to carry this advance through with two mobile columns.'

He decided that each column would consist of a tank battalion, an infantry battalion and a motor-cycle infantry company (4 RNF). The first objective was to be the line of the River Cojeul and the second the Sensée around Vis-en-Artois. A more detailed plan simply could not be made due to a lack of information and time available for the tanks' and the infantry's battle procedure.

Just before 0700 hours, this plan was quickly imparted to the two brigade commanders: Brigadiers Pratt, 1 Tank Brigade; and Churchill of 151 Brigade. The Left Column, taking the inside track around Arras, was to be principally 4 RTR and 6 DLI, and the outer or Right Column 7 RTR and 8 DLI. The force's reserve was to be 9 DLI and the remainder of 4 RNF, who were to follow on behind the columns with Brigade HQ.

The infantry battalion commanding officers were nominated as the commanders of the two columns. Unfortunately, rather than regrouping into columns around Vimy with orders and coordinating instructions being given by the two DLI commanding officers to both tank and infantry sub-unit commanders, the two brigade commanders returned to their troops and gave orders separately. A vital element of battle procedure had failed and had repercussions throughout the day. Without the tank battalion COs being present at the column commanders' orders, there was an inevitable divergence of view regarding aims and the concept of operations.

There is also an abiding suspicion that the infantry, never having seen a tank let alone trained with them, were happy to go their own way and that Brigadiers Pratt and Pope, having good reason to be suspicious of the way non-armoured commanders had hitherto tried or been forced to use tanks in the campaign so far, were only too happy to concur. There is another suspicion, which is that the Regular Army commanding officers of the two RTR battalions were reluctant to operate too closely under the command of Territorials!

The regrouping, however, of a battery of 2-pounders from the 5th Division's 52nd Anti-Tank Regiment to the Left Column successfully took place in the concentration area on Vimy Ridge.

Left Column:
Lieutenant Colonel T.H. Miller
4th Battalion, Royal Tank Regiment
Lieutenant Colonel Fitzmaurice
7 x Matilda, 23 x Mk I & 5 Light Tanks
6th Battalion, Durham light Infantry
206th Anti-Tank Battery RA (from 52nd Anti-Tank Regiment RA, 2-
    pounders)

Diagram of a 1940 version of the 2-pounder.

368th Field Battery RA (from 92nd Field Regiment RA, 25-pounders)
A platoon of 151st Brigade Anti-Tank Company
Y Company, 4th Battalion, Royal Northumberland Fusiliers
1 scout platoon, 4th Battalion, Royal Northumberland Fusiliers

Right Flank Protection
X Company, 4th Battalion, Royal Northumberland Fusiliers (remainder)

Right Column
Lieutenant Colonel C.W. Bean
7th Battalion, Royal Tank Regiment
Lieutenant Colonel Heyland
9 x Matilda, 35 x Mk I & 4 Light Tanks
8th Battalion, Durham Light Infantry
260th Anti-Tank Battery RA (from 65th Anti-Tank Regiment RA,
    2-pounders)
365th Field Battery RA (from 92nd Field Regiment RA, 18-pounders)
A platoon of 151st Brigade Anti-Tank Company
Z Company, 4th Battalion, Royal Northumberland Fusiliers (withdrawn into
    reserve)
1 scout platoon, 4th Battalion, Royal Northumberland Fusiliers

Reserve
9th Battalion, Durham Light Infantry

The Germans reach the coast.

Time was short and General Martel requested a delay in H-Hour from 1400 to 1500 hours but General Franklyn initially turned down any delay.

The Germans

The news of the previous evening that Guderian had reached the coast at Abbeville, cutting off the First Army Group, had prompted another bout of hesitancy in the German chain of command from Berlin downwards. Consequently, Rommel's spearhead, along with the rest of Hoth's XV Panzer Corps among others, were again halted until further notice. During the course of the night and into the 21st, with the forward troops having been halted, those further back and in the formations following the panzer spearheads were given the opportunity to catch up during the night of 20/21 May and into the following morning. These following formations included the *SS Totenkopf* Division who had been in action on Rommel's right rear during 20 May.

The Air Support Issue

During the preceding days, for very good reasons, the majority of the Royal Air Force (RAF) had redeployed back to airfields in southern England from where its remaining aircraft would henceforth operate. The only British RAF element still in France was a part of the Advanced Air Striking Force with three fighter squadrons and six bomber squadrons but these were located well south of the German breakthrough and were supporting the French. With liaison and communication between the RAF and GHQ in France further degraded by the move back to the UK, command and control (C2) arrangements for the bomber squadrons allocated to support the BEF were at this point ad hoc to say the least. C2 was now being exercised directly from the Air Ministry without reference to Lord Gort and the BEF's Headquarters staff.

In ordering fifty-seven Blenheim bomber sorties for 21 May, principally to the north-west of Arras, the Air Ministry was working on information based on air recce sorties flown at dawn that day and only reported transport and south of Arras marching infantry. The lack of movement was due to the panzers, following their stunning success in reaching the Channel coast the previous day, not being permitted to resume their advance until the afternoon. Consequently, with no panzers to be seen by air recce and the impossibility of getting information about Frankforce's operation back to the Air Ministry, there was to be no RAF air support to the coming operation.

The 12th Lancers
While battle preparations for the attack were under way, early on 21 May the 12th Lancers were already deployed to the west and north-west of Arras. B Squadron headed west and found there was still a considerable number of panzers and other vehicles in Avesnes (8th Panzer Division). C Squadron was stopped on the St. Pol road about 3 miles out of Arras due to the volume of refugees and French and Belgian military transport.

RAF bombs fall on Abbeville Airfield, 21 May 1940.

German 150mm sFH 18 Feldhaubitze in action.

The hilltop abbey at Mont-St. Eloi, destroyed during the First World War but used as the HQ location for 12th Lancers.

Once they had cleared the refugee traffic, a troop from C Squadron was halted to confer over a map when a German battery of 150mm guns was seen moving towards them on the road. It was immediately engaged at close quarters, destroying the battery and taking prisoners. This was almost certainly a part of the 3rd Battalion, 80th Artillery Regiment.

Across their area of operations, the 12th Lancers' patrols encountered scattered enemy units on the roads to the south and west of Arras and in the St. Pol area. Many were engaged and prisoners of war were taken; these were, of course, a problem for armoured cars.

The Lancers' RHQ deployed to the excellent viewing point of Mont-St. Eloi (wrongly spelt as Eloy on British maps) during the day but redeployed when the 3rd DLM moved into the area during the afternoon. Throughout the day the regiment's recce patrols were able to report an accurate picture of what was going on to their front but sadly, such was the dislocation of the chain of command and the ad hoc nature of Frankforce, little of this information reached any level of command in time to be useful.

Prepare to March
The two tank battalions of 1 Army Tank Brigade arrived at Vimy in the early hours, having lost about 25 per cent of their tank strength due to breakdown. With only a few hours for rest and maintenance, further breakdowns could be expected. Lieutenant Colonel Fitzmaurice's 4 RTR had thirty-five Infantry Tank Mk Is mounting a single machine gun and a two-man crew, plus six Mk VI Light Tanks. 7 RTR under Lieutenant Colonel Heyland had twenty-three Mk I tanks and sixteen Infantry Tank Mk IIs (Matildas), armed with a 2-pounder gun and manned by a crew of four. The two battalions totalled 83 tanks: 16 Matildas, 58 Mk Is and the 9 Mk VI Light Tanks. Brigadier Pratt ordered seven Matildas under Major Herdwick's command to be transferred to 4 RTR to balance the strength of the two columns.

There were only seventy-five minutes for battle procedure, which consisted of briefings from battalion down to section level, preparation of weapons, ammunition and equipment, plus feeding. In the case of the 6 DLI, they were attempting to give the men a hot meal but time was too short and such food as was available was issued as haversack rations but, even then, not all of the companies received them.

The only eventual compromise over H-Hour was that for the tanks it would remain at 1400 hours but for the infantry, 'if they could make it', it would be 1430. It was also settled that the start line would be the Arras-Doullens railway, which was to be crossed by the tanks at H-Hour.

Rushing the tanks forward and into action and accepting that the infantry would not be there with them on the start line at H-Hour demonstrates not only the degree of pressure that General Martel and his brigadiers were under to get

British infantrymen: battle preparations. Boys anti-tank gun and a Bren gun being cleaned.

moving, but also how weak was the concept of the all-arms battle in 1940. 'Gun Buster' will reveal that this was also the case with the columns' artillery.

Radio silence was to be maintained and sets only turned on and netted in on the start line. As we will see, any tactical benefit that this communication security measure might have yielded was outweighed by the consequences of a lack of communication on the march to the start line.

The gunners of 368 Battery, however, having been regrouped from the 5th Division, would, it appears, have had no such instructions or had missed them in the rushed orders process. Yet their communications were working well as they left the concentration area on the first leg of their march to a hide in the Anzin-St. Aubin area.

Chapter 6

March to the Start Line

The first stage of the operation was the assembly of the various units and sub-units that were to make up the two columns and the brigade reserve, at Marœuil for the Right Column and Anzin-St. Aubin for the Left. However, things went wrong from the start. The majority of the motorcyclists of Z Company, 4th Royal Northumberland Fusiliers (Right Column) were not ready to march and eventually joined the brigade reserve. Without the services of Z Company, it was left to the remaining Mk VI Light Tanks of the Scout Platoon to help maintain a tenuous link between 7 RTR and the marching infantry of 8 DLI in this column. Z Company, less their Scout Platoon, joined 9 DLI as part of the Brigade Reserve.

Lieutenant Tom Craig of 7 RTR summed up the state of the tanks as they left Petit Vimy at 1145 hours, at the beginning of his battalion's move to the start line in what was a rushed and ill-prepared operation:

> I arrived at Petit Vimy in my Matilda exhausted and disorganised. I was given a map by my squadron commander and told to start up and follow him. The wireless was not working, there was no tie-up with the infantry and no clear orders. That was our state as we crossed the start point on our way to our first action.

Lieutenant Tom Craig (centre) as CO in the 1960s.

The Germans

General Hoth's plan for the XV Panzer Corps on 21 May, once the advance was allowed to resume, was for the 7th Panzer Division to swing west of Arras and head to objectives astride the River Scarpe to the north-west of the city. The 5th Panzer Division was to the east of the Arras-Cambrai road heading north, to the right rear of Rommel's division. Their task was to fix the Arras defences and screen the 7th Panzer's move west. On the Corps' open left flank, the motorized *SS Totenkopf* Division had moved up overnight from Cambrai and would attempt to keep pace with Rommel.

While the British columns prepared to march from the Vimy area to their assembly areas and start lines, Rommel and the *SS Totenkopf* had finally been given permission to resume their march and Rommel wrote:

At about 14.00 hours [German time was +1 hour] I gave the Panzer Regiment orders to attack. Although the armour had by this time been seriously reduced in numbers, due to breakdowns and casualties, this was a model of what an attack should be. When I saw the weight of it I

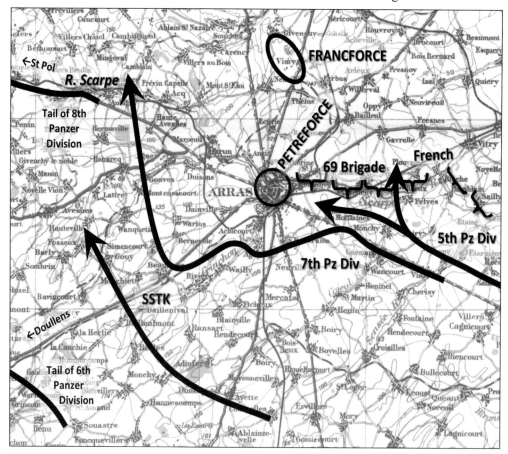

The German plan for 21 May 1940.

Rommel gives orders during the campaign in France.

was convinced that the 7th Panzer Division's new thrust into enemy territory would be as successful as all the other actions of the preceding days. I had actually intended to accompany the tanks again myself, together with Lieutenant Most, my dispatch riders, armoured car and signals vehicle, and to conduct operations from there by wireless.

The panzer spearheads, having tangled with and disposed of a handful of French tanks at Vis-en-Artois, were soon well ahead of the infantry regiments. Skirting around Arras, 25th Panzer Regiment headed north-west, making use of roads where they ran in the right direction, and where they didn't, cutting across the open country. Having crossed le Gy Rau stream [this name taken from the map used on the day of battle] around Agnez-lès-Duisans, the panzers had just reached the Scarpe between Aubigny-en-Artois and Arc and were waiting for the infantry, who were by now some 6 miles to the rear, to catch up. Here they sat until word of a problem behind them was finally received at approximately 1700 hours.

Rommel's 25th Panzer Regiment had taken a broad swing to the west, almost following the route taken by the 8th Panzer Division the day before, intending to be sufficiently far from Arras to avoid tangling with the city's defences. Thus the panzers were not to run headlong into the British armour marching in the opposite direction to its start lines. As it was, the two sides just missed each other in both time and distance.

Left Column

In contrast to Lieutenant Craig's experience, Lieutenant Peter Vaux, 4 RTR's recce officer, had few problems. Leading the Left Column, he was mounted in one of four remaining light tanks in his troop:

> In the approach march to this attack 4 RTR had no serious problems. The reason is as follows: before the War we had been Army Motorcycling champions, and had a very strong motorcycling spirit in the Regiment. Thus our dispatch riders were of a very high standard. Throughout our march from south of Brussels back to our assembly area, those dispatch riders and the recce officers of the squadrons put us bang on the Start Line at the right place and in spite of the disruptions.
>
> There were no cockups such as I observed later in the war. Despite a certain amount of shot and shell, no-one got off the axis and we all ended up in the right place. My only recollection of the march from Petit Vimy to Dainville is that we had one long stop. The Squadron Leader took the opportunity of calling us to an O [Orders] Group in a farmhouse where we were lucky enough to get some coffee and a bit of rum, and the opportunity to have a look at a map. I well remember trying to make a mental picture of the whole line of advance onto the objective.
>
> Some French tanks about 3 kilometres back passed us on our left. I do remember that we were told we were going to be supported by the French but they disappeared and I never saw them again.
>
> So from my eyes the approach march had no problems. It was very slow and had many stoppages but right up to the Start Line there were no problems at all.

Even so, it was not an easy march. There were very few maps available, and the roads were jammed with refugees' abandoned vehicles and carts. Cross-country movement was also severely hampered by quite a number of First World War trenches that had yet to be filled in.

With time for battle preparations being tight as a result of General Franklyn being forced to bring the operation forward, it had all been very rushed for the infantry, with battle procedure being heavily curtailed and few in the rifle companies had more than the vaguest notion of what the plan was and their part in it. While the tanks had netted in their radios several days before, the infantry of 151 Brigade could only do so once they reached their assembly areas.

Mark VI Light Tank.

Refugees take cover from strafing by the Luftwaffe.

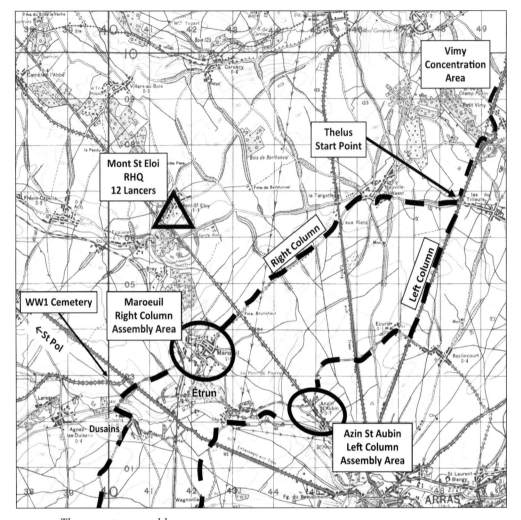

Vimy
Concentration
Area

Thelus
Start Point

Mont St Eloi
RHQ
12 Lancers

Right Column

Left Column

WW1 Cemetery

Maroeuil
Right Column
Assembly Area

St Pol

Étrun

Dusains

Azin St Aubin
Left Column
Assembly Area

ARRAS

The move to assembly areas.

At 1130 hours, 6 DLI eventually passed the start point of their approach march at Thélus crossroads, with Major Peter Jeffreys, the battalion's second-in-command, forward with D Company. This was an 8-mile march to the start line, to the railway where the operation south of Arras was due to begin.

At about the same time, 'Gun Buster', Battery Captain of 368 Battery, led a column of some twelve guns and vehicles out onto the *route nationale*, up over the ridge from Vimy and down onto the plain beyond heading to the assembly area at Anzin-St. Aubin:

At half-past ten the Battery pulled out of positions and took the Lens-Arras road over the left side of Vimy Ridge towards Arras. At the village of Écurie, a mile and a half from Arras, we branched off to the right. In front we could hear the bursting shells and bombs, the rattle of machine-guns, and scattered rifle fire, where the grim struggle for

Arras was raging. Over Arras itself hung a thick pall of smoke, very distinct and sombre against the wide sweep of the sky's otherwise flawless blue.

The Major had proceeded ahead with the infantry commander, taking along our Wagon-Lincs officer whose job it was to find us a 'hide' in the vicinity of the village of Anzin-St. Aubin. Here the Battery was to meet him. This morning the main road was surprisingly clear of fugitives. The flood had exhausted itself at last, and the troops could now move forward unhampered. A regiment of French cuirassiers (mechanized, with four-seater cars, and motor-cycle combinations carrying machine-guns) were halted by the roadside, and on the outskirts of a ruined village a British motor-cycle machine-gun battalion [4 RNF] was waiting to go into action.

We climbed a small rise into Anzin-St. Aubin where the Wagon-Lines Officer met us. ...He had (he said) found us the ideal 'hide'. ... Proudly he led us into the grounds of a deserted château [it is today the Marie] encircled by a broad drive, tree-lined on both sides.

The place had evidently only recently been vacated. ...It made a very pretty picture. But the picture would have been much prettier if we hadn't seen three unmistakable shell-holes in the lawn. They were as ominous as Man Friday's footprints.

The Right Column

The route from Petit Vimy took 7 RTR over the ridge on the *route nationale* and down towards the start point for the march at the crossroads outside Thélus, which then, as now, are dominated by a large French memorial. Here, taking the outer or right-hand route, they turned off towards Neuville-St. Vaast. Progress at first was straightforward, but descending into Marœuil and the valley of the River Scarpe their difficulties multiplied. Map-reading, for those who had maps, was confusing in the maze of village streets.

As the head of 7 RTR's column crested the rise north of Marœuil they also came under artillery fire but suffered no casualties. However, as they threaded their way through the village they ran into small groups of German troops at the bridges over the Scarpe in Marœuil and in Étrun. These are thought to be the remnants of the 150mm battery, following behind 8th Panzer Division taken on by the 12th Lancers the previous evening.

Marching on foot already some way behind 7 RTR

the advance guard of 8 DLI reached Marœuil at 1245 hours; the composition was A Company of 8 DLI with the Scout Troop of Z Company 4th Northumberland Fusiliers on their motorcycles. The Carrier Platoon, less a section; then followed Battalion HQ with the CO and behind that the Mortar Platoon and behind that B, C and D Companies in that order.

The pause by the tanks in the assembly area at Marœuil allowed the infantry to catch up. Here in the village Lieutenant Colonel Bean met Major General Martel, who had come forward to see what was going on and was also able to talk briefly with Lieutenant Colonel Heyland, CO of 7 RTR, who 'reported that he had some tanks missing. After that he went off about his business and we never saw him again.' Major Ian English of 8 DLI recalled:

> Soon after that the tank Liaison Officer, who was in a scout car, came to the CO and reported that he had lost wireless contact with his CO, so in fact we had no communication with the tanks apart from running across and talking to them. To add to our troubles, the Battery Commander of our supporting artillery [365 Battery] came to the CO and said that he was having difficulty in getting up into a position where they could support the advance because of the congestion on the roads, and the CO said 'You'll just have to get on with it.' In spite of that we didn't have any artillery support during the course of the day.

Major English went on to comment that the enemy artillery was clearly having no such deployment or communication difficulties: 'In Marœuil the Germans were shelling occasionally – they weren't causing very much trouble – and there was some light automatic fire coming over from a wood on the south-east of the village.'

Being further away from Arras, on the outer route both 7 RTR and 8 DLI found refugees and isolated French units were still plentiful and caused an impediment.

Meanwhile the leading squadrons, having crossed the Scarpe bridges and driven on through Étrun, brushed with and engaged enemy logistic transport on the St. Pol road. Lieutenant Tom Craig mounted in a Matilda had followed his Squadron HQ into Duisans: 'On approaching DUISANS there was the sound of firing from leading tanks and we deployed astride the road. Many German vehicles were burning, troop carriers with infantry were moving West on the road and we engaged them successfully. We were ordered to cross the main road.'

Major English, following at the head of 8 DLI column, described the scene and the ample evidence of the passage of 7 RTR and/or French tanks a short while earlier:

> We arrived at the junction [north of Duisans] – it was a hot day and the men were tired. They were hot and sweaty, having had little rest, with sore feet, for we had not done much marching training; they were fed up and probably anxious, because they knew they were about to go into action for the first time. At the junction we saw quite a number of burning trucks and a few dead Germans about. One truck was on its side,

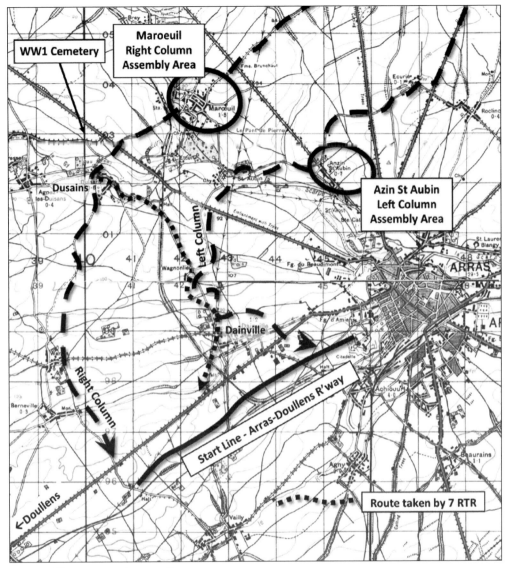

The route to the start line.

with the general appearance of the chaos of war, with shells and equipment and steel helmets lying about. We realised that this German column had been shot up. The effect was remarkable. The chaps said 'By Jove, this is good, perhaps it's worth it after all.' There were some German prisoners in the hands of some French tank men.

Just up the St. Pol road is a 1914–1918 War Cemetery. Soon after we got into that position a French Tank Commander came to us and said that there were a lot of Germans holding the cemetery, and that he would like us to go and rout them out.

C Company Commander was in two minds what to do. Our orders had been that the advance must go forward as briskly as possible and he didn't want to get diverted. Anyway the French officer persuaded him and they went off with them along with the Battalion intelligence officer and French interpreter, who was a Sergeant.

C Company advanced on the area of the cemetery with the French tanks providing liberal fire support from their machine guns. There was little resistance from the enemy; they took thirty prisoners and collected as many dead and wounded from around the gravestones. Major English recalled that 'The French made them strip to their pants and made them lie down in the road. Eventually they got dressed and we had them sent back to Battalion HQ.'

There have been certain revisionist claims of atrocities committed here by C Company. Taking into account a possible untidy transition from the hot blood and fear of delivering an attack to the cool legal position of dealing with enemy wounded and prisoners of war, there is no war crime that can be laid at the feet of the DLI at the cemetery.

Up ahead, Lieutenant Tom Craig, still following his squadron commander, was on the move out of Duisans:

> I followed on towards DAINVILLE: just north of the village we came under spasmodic shellfire, and I remember negotiating the HT wires which had fallen across the road on the northern outskirts of the village. We passed through the village without opposition, turned left on the main road and then right towards ACHICOURT.

Leaving Duisans, 7 RTR had incorrectly taken one of the roads south-east instead of bypassing the village to the west on the nominated route. This deviation towards Achicourt rather than Warlus is unexplained. The presence of enemy on the St. Pol road, as already recounted, could have forced them off their route or it could have been a simple navigation error in the maze of roads in Marœuil, Étrun and Duisans (easily done!), exacerbated by a lack of maps; one mistake and all the rest followed! There is speculation as to what would have happened if 7 RTR had followed its correct route towards Warlus, where they could have brushed with the flank of a battalion of 25th Panzer Regiment as they headed north. The assertion is that with the panzers unable to knock out the British tanks and the Matilda's 2-pounder gun being able to take on the light German tanks, this could have been a British success. However, the facts argue differently! With 7 RTR, no artillery support, a long way forward of 206 Anti-Tank Battery, only having nine Matildas armed with 2-pounders and the Mk I tanks armed only with machine guns, 25th Panzer Regiment, with approximately 100 serviceable tanks, would have been able to overwhelm the forty-eight British tanks.

Further back Colonel Bean had now established Battalion Headquarters in the château on the outskirts of Duisans and before long more German prisoners were brought in, this time taken by a platoon of B Company in some scrub around the village. The enemy that 8 DLI were encountering were probably either the tail of the 8th Panzer Division or remnants of the logistic elements following up behind 25th Panzer Regiment encountered earlier on the St. Pol road.

About this time Brigadier Pratt of 1 Army Tank Brigade encountered the roving General Martel and told him: 'This is going to be a cock-up, the infantry are miles behind. We are going forward against strong opposition and we know it's around. We will be absolutely smashed and we must stop this mess, get things together and try later.'

General Martel, fully aware of the wider situation and under pressure from General Franklyn to get forward quickly, replied that the attack must go ahead. With the state of radio communications across the force, it was unlikely to have been able to be stopped anyway as events were generating their own momentum.

Right Flank

Out on the right flank, beyond 7 RTR and 8 DLI, French troops were not yet in sight but 12th Lancers' OP on Mont-St. Eloi and their patrols on the ground saw 25th Panzer Regiment making its wide swing to the north-west of Arras. A motorcyclist of X Company, 4 RNF's Scout Platoon, deployed south-west of Duisans, also spotted them and eventually a message reached Headquarters 151 Brigade that enemy armour had been seen. However, the Scout Platoon, isolated on the right flank, was eventually overrun by the panzers and destroyed out towards Wanquetin. The remainder of X Company was withdrawn to less exposed positions back with 9 DLI in reserve. With radio communications to the forward troops barely working, there is no evidence that this information reached the tanks.

Colonel Bean and the French troops from the 3rd DLM that they had fallen in with around Duisans were by now, not unnaturally, concerned about German activity on their right flank following their various contacts with the enemy. Consequently, the commanding officer ordered a troop of 2-pounder guns of 260 (Norfolk Yeomanry) Anti-Tank Battery to be deployed into a screen to cover the right or western flank.

In their first proper action, with the gunners fully expecting to be engaging the enemy, tanks appeared to their front just a short while later. The two sides opened fire on each other but after several minutes it was realized that the 'attacking' tanks were in fact French. With poor armoured fighting vehicle recognition skills, a lack of briefing on the French presence on the right flanks and the excitement of a first action, friendly fire inevitably resulted.

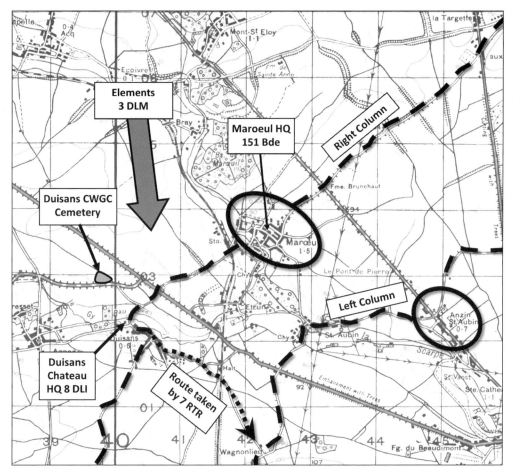

First encounters with the enemy.

7 RTR

The now well 'off-route' tanks of 7 RTR, as they approached Dainville, ran into the rear of 4 RTR's column and the head of 6 DLI's, causing further confusion in the tank battalion. Brigadier Pope had crossed the Scarpe and made his way forward to Dainville in order to meet General Martel and Brigadier Pratt, who were to have set up their tactical headquarters there. As he entered the village he came across the commanding officer of 7 RTR, Lieutenant Colonel Heyland, 'in a state of some excitement, having completely lost himself. His Battalion and he himself had come in too far to the left, and I formed the impression that he was not in control of his unit at all.'

Without radio communication there was little he could do other than drive himself and other officers in light tanks around gathering groups of tanks and ordering them to follow the obvious pylon line back to the Doullens road and the railway line beyond. 7 RTR in the lead of the Right Column were as a result late starting their part in the operation but at approximately this time the leading

A 2-pounder gun deployed for action.

two companies of 8 DLI were still 2 miles further back, between Duisans and Warlus.

8 DLI
With the tanks having headed to the south-east and Dainville, 8 DLI on the correct route south to Warlus were soon in action against Germans who had not already been disrupted by the tanks. Major English continued his account:

> At about 3 pm the Advance Guard ran into opposition south of Duisans on the road on the open ground over on your half right, and the CO ordered D Company to come forward to support the Advance Guard in the further advance.
> General Martel turned up again and wondered what all the hold-up was about and asked why weren't we getting on quicker. The CO explained the position and soon after that we continued the advance to Warlus.

Now that 8 DLI were out of the close country between Marœuil and Duisans and into open farmland, without tank support and with increasing reports of enemy activity to the right and front, Colonel Bean decided that B and C companies, the former having cleared Duisans and the latter having returned from their clearance of the St. Pol road, were to take up temporary defensive positions in the village under the leadership of the battalion's second-in-command. Their task was to act as a firm base, which would also serve to protect his right rear. Once Warlus was secured it was intended that they were to move forward and join the rest of the column.

A and D companies along with the Carrier Platoon and Battalion Headquarters set out on their advance to Warlus, 2 miles further to the south, where the situation developed into a battle:

> Between Duisans and Warlus we saw quite a number of German tanks away over on our right and also some German infantry digging in. The CO decided we needed more anti-tank support so he told the Battery Commander to bring up another troop. Unfortunately, that troop never arrived. On the way up it saw some tanks away on their right and they had a battle with them and three or four of the German tanks were at least damaged but another one knocked out one of our guns and the troop never reached us on our way to Warlus.

368 Battery: Left Column

The battery had not been in its hide at Anzin-St. Aubin for long when a couple of shells passed overhead, detonating 100 yards beyond. 'Gun Buster' recalled: 'In rapid succession a dozen more shells swished over our heads, all bursting in the same field. Then we had peace again. But I hoped we should soon be on the move. This château looked too much like a registered target to be comfortable.'

He didn't have long to wait as he was called to the battery command post:

> 'We're going into action,' came the Major's [battery commander's] voice. 'I want you, the CPO [Command Post Officer] and his assistant, and the Gun Position Officers [GPO] to meet me without delay at the first cross-roads at Dainville. Gun groups will remain in their present "hide". Got it?'
>
> I repeated back, dashed out of the truck and shouted 'Orders!' The other officers and the senior sergeants gathered around and we studied the maps.
>
> 'Any questions?' I asked. 'No? Then off we go.'
>
> At the crossroads the Major emerged from a wayside barn looking rather shaken up.
>
> 'Anything wrong, sir?' I asked.

Just as the battery commander had reached Dainville, the enemy started to heavily shell the village. He had taken cover in a barn, where a shell exploded on the roof above him, 'bowling him over. As he went down something whizzed right past his ear. "And here it is," he added, reverently producing from his pocket the nose of a shell.'

The infantry had, however, gone on ahead to the start line and into battle without being able to contact their gunners. With neither gunners nor tanks in the 50th Division's normal order of battle before the war or during the Phoney War, the DLI were acting as their training and experience had taught them as independent infantry battalions. It proved to be beyond the capability of either of the brigade commanders, Pratt and Churchill, to coordinate movement in an uncertain situation with very poor communications. 'Gun Buster's' battery commander's orders exemplify the problem: 'The 6th Battalion of the Blankshires [6 DLI] are in front. Get off to their Battalion Headquarters. You'll probably find them somewhere on the road towards Achicourt.'

9 DLI

The task of 9 DLI, nominated as Brigade Reserve for Phase One of the operation, was to follow the 8th Battalion and to protect the right flank of the advance. Lieutenant Colonel Percy wrote:

> I had under my command, for this role, a battery of Anti-tank guns, some sappers and a company of 4th Royal Northumberland Fusiliers (Motor Cycle Bn.)… My orders were to advance by stages, under the direction of Bde. H.Q., and we remained some time, at first in a village called Neuville-St. Vaast, where we were bombed. Here we saw some of our heavy tanks, which had been damaged, coming out of action. They seemed to have stood up to direct hits by German Anti-tank guns very well. Orders came to move to the next village, Marœuil, a few miles east of Arras. The road we took ran along a ridge overlooking the area in which the other two battalions were advancing and it was a clear, sunny afternoon.

9 DLI's main task was to have been in Phase Two but this, of course, was not to take place.

Chapter 7

The Left Column's Battle

4 RTR reached its start line on time at 1400 hours, where there was some delay before crossing the railway line as the level crossing gates were closed. Railway lines were considered to be very much of an obstacle to the tanks of 1940 and with deeply-ingrained training not to damage property, there was a pause! Eventually, there were instructions 'to drive through the bloody thing' and a light tank did the deed.

On the battalion's right, however, C Squadron's leading tanks, despite concerns that it might be electrified, started to cross the railway but it was a slow process and not all managed to get across, with some tanks becoming stuck on rails and in some places steep embankments or cuttings, most of which would cause little problem to the tanks of just a few years later.

Shaking out into formation, two squadrons abreast, the tanks climbed onto a slight crest and straight into the flank of the 1st Battalion, 6th Rifle Regiment of the 7th Panzer Division. The trucks carrying the German infantry had turned south-east out of Agny and were strung out down the road D3 to Wailly following at least 6 miles behind in the wake of the 25th Panzer Regiment.

Second Lieutenant Peter Vaux recalled:

We had come straight into the flank of a German mechanised column which was moving across our front. They were just as surprised as us, because they were in the trees, and we were immediately right in amongst them. And for some quarter of an hour or so there was a glorious 'free for all'. We knocked out quite a lot of their lorries; there were Germans running all over the place.

Brigadier Douglas Pratt, Commander 1 Army Tank Brigade, wrote in a letter penned shortly after the battle, even though he personally was not forward with 4 RTR:

We got about four miles forward before any infantry of ours appeared in sight. During this time, we played hell with a lot of Boche motor transport and their kindred stuff. Tracer ammunition put a lot up in flames. His anti-tank gunners, after firing a bit, bolted and left their guns,

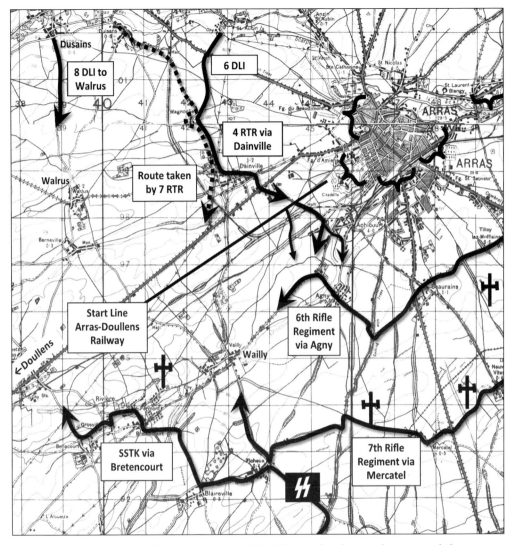

The move of 6th Rifle Regiment and the SS Totenkopf around Arras and the clash with 4 RTR.

even when fired on at ranges of 600 to 800 yards with machine-guns from Matildas. Some surrendered, and others feigned dead on the ground!

Brigadier Pope was also watching from a vantage point at the Arras racecourse to the north of Dainville:

There was a slight haze which made detailed observation difficult, but it did my heart good to see the manner in which the Brigade went into action. There was a good deal of machine-gun and anti-tank gunfire,

German transport, probably commandeered from civilian use. It has an Iserlohn number plate, not a military 'WH'.

more than I expected, but the tanks pushed on without faltering and as they passed the fire was subdued.

The German infantry were panicked by the eruption of British armour on their flank and did their best to escape. Many, however, attempted to surrender but tanks without infantry cannot effectively take prisoners and therefore many Germans who surrendered subsequently 'went to ground' as the British tanks passed by and lived to fight another day. If there had even been a small number of DLI infantry who could have ridden on the tanks to the start line, the story and impact of this encounter may have been more serious for the Germans and also more long-lasting.

However, without properly working radio communication across the battalion, control of the squadrons and even troops was difficult; tank commanders fought almost independent actions. Even so, Lieutenant Vaux recalled that 'we had a highly successful battle. I don't know how many German vehicles we set on fire. At that moment we did not see why we shouldn't go all the way to Berlin.'

With their tails up, 4 RTR drove on through the enemy, with A and B squadrons heading left towards Achicourt and their Phase One objective on the River Cojeul beyond, while on the right C Squadron pushed on towards Agny.

Thus far the battle had been one-sided but surprise was not the only thing that 4 RTR had going for it. Brigadier Pratt wrote:

None of his anti-tank stuff penetrated our Mk Is or IIs and nor even did his field artillery which fired high explosive. Some tracks were broken and a few tanks were put on fire by his tracer bullets, chiefly in the engine compartment of the Mark Is. One Matilda had fourteen direct hits from enemy 37mm guns and it had no harmful effect, just gouged out a bit of armour!

German 37mm Pak 36 anti-tank gun, nicknamed the 'Door knocker' or 'Panzerknocker'.

Mark I tank.

As we will see, Brigadier Pratt was correct about the inadequacies of the 37mm gun but direct fire from German 105mm field artillery was to contribute significantly to the outcome of both RTR battalions' attacks.

Troop commander WO 3 Armit's experience in his Mk I tank bears out the Germans' inability to penetrate the armour of the Mk I or the Matilda with the 37mm. He advanced under heavy anti-tank fire, engaging with his .50 Vickers machine gun which soon jammed. Consequently, with no effective weapon, he used the tank, charging the line of six deployed 37mm anti-tank guns. The German gun crews managed to get one gun away, while the remainder of the gunners ran off. Armit, ably supported by Sergeant Strickland, drove over the remainder of the abandoned guns, crushing them under their tracks. As a result of the 1940 campaign the 37mm earned the nickname the 'Panzer Knocker' among the German anti-tank gunners. Its inability

Colonel Miller in the First World War.

to knock out the heavier Allied tanks in 1940 was the spur to develop much better tank and anti-tank guns which demonstrably gave the Germans the edge in this field later in the war.

Some 3 miles further back Lieutenant Colonel Miller of 6 DLI could hear the tanks in action and, having fought alongside tanks in the First World War, knew that any ground gained would have to be secured and held by his infantry. Therefore he urged his very tired and footsore men onwards towards the sound of battle.

Hurrying along in the wake of the tanks the Durhams started to arrive on the scene of 4 RTR's action south of Dainville. Remarking on the aftermath of the tanks' encounter with 6th Rifle Regiment, Major Jeffreys recalled

> we found a lot of German dead and took a lot of prisoners. They came forward surrendering and very correct they were. I remember a German officer came up to me and he said, 'Are you the senior officer around here?' in broken English. 'Yes,' I said. He replied 'I would like to personally surrender to you.' 'Well,' I said, 'you can do what you like,' and he replied 'I and my men would like to lay down our arms and surrender.' 'Alright, throw down all your stuff there. Give me your map,' and I handed them over to a Lance Corporal to take back and off we went.

B Company was dispatched to follow C Squadron on the right towards Agny, while C and D companies followed A and B squadrons towards Achicourt, but in an attempt to remain in contact with 4 RTR Colonel Miller sent his Carrier Platoon on ahead. A Company was the battalion reserve.

Ahead of them with both the villages of Achicourt and Beaurains under

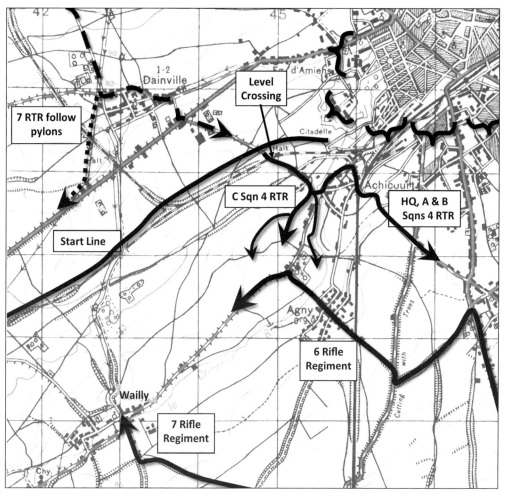

4 RTR's battle with 6th and 7th Rifle Regiments.

artillery fire, A Squadron, 4 RTR with B Squadron and Colonel Fitzmaurice's Regimental Headquarters following made best speed through them, passing some French tanks that were already in action. As the leading British tanks emerged into open country south-east of Arras they were engaged by panzers. These were either stragglers from Rommel's division or elements of the 5th Panzer Division's advance guard. German Recce troops were normally reinforced with a *panzerspitz* (panzer armoured spearhead) of a tank platoon.

Having cut their way through the 2nd Battalion, 6th Rifle Regiment, 4 RTR now encountered the 7th Panzer Division's artillery. Lieutenant Vaux recalled:

> We went over this hill, and as we came across the top, I remember down below there was a very large German tank with a big gun and we had nothing that would deal with that, and so the Colonel called across to

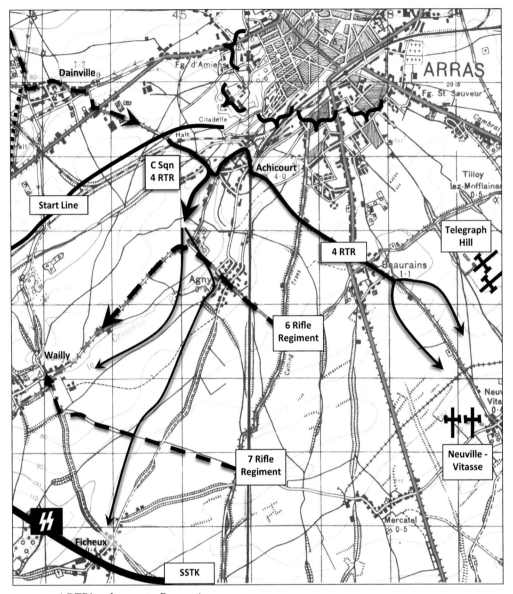

4 RTR's advance to Beaurains.

me and said, 'Go back to the cemetery [Beaurains] where that French
tank is and ask him to come up and deal with this German.' …Well, I
went back there and I drew alongside the Frenchman and he opened the
hatch in the side of his tank and said, 'What do you want?' and I told
him, and he said, 'Oh, I can't come, I am very busy, I am shooting into
this cemetery.' Why he was shooting into it I don't know, because I
couldn't see anybody to provide a target. However, while I was arguing
with him there was a sudden burst of firing and some shells fell around

us and he shouted, 'Attention! Attention!' slammed the door and motored off ... So I got back into my tank, turned around and went back the way I had come. Well, when I got back I found in fact that the German tank had disappeared – which was very convenient of him – and I looked down the valley and what a sight I saw!

Meanwhile, as 4 RTR had continued to move on from Beaurains towards the Cambrai road with A and B squadrons deployed and the CO's tank in the centre, they were engaged by enemy 105mm guns. These were the three batteries of Rommel's 2nd Battalion, 78th Artillery Regiment emplaced on Telegraph Hill,

German 105mm Leichte Feldhaubitze 18 with the gun barrel at full recoil having just fired.

covering the division's swing around Arras to the west. Lieutenant Vaux returned from his abortive mission but what had happened while he was away was not immediately apparent to him:

> I could see…upwards of twenty tanks, down in the valley just short of a potato clamp. The Colonel's tank was down there, a little in front of them – I could see it quite clearly, it was stationary with the flag flying from it. The Adjutant's tank was quite close to the Colonel's, but from where I was I wasn't quite sure what to do, so I called up the Colonel to tell him about the French tank. I called and I called and I called, but I got no answer, and then the Adjutant came on the air and he just said, 'Come over and join me.' So I motored down to the valley and as I did so I saw the Adjutant drive forward to the area of the potato clamp and start shooting, and as I got closer I saw that there were German anti-tank guns in the area with their crews running about. At that time, a good deal of fire was coming from the area of the wood on Telegraph Hill and it was very heavy fire from field-guns; much heavier than anything we had encountered so far.
>
> I went forward through the tanks of A Squadron and I thought it very strange that they weren't moving and they weren't shooting, and then I noticed that there was something even odder about them – their guns were pointing at all angles; a lot of them had their turret hatches open and some of the crews were half in and half out of the tanks, lying wounded or dead. I realised then, with a shock, that all these twenty tanks had been knocked out by those big guns.
>
> In the grass, I could see a number of black berets as the crews were crawling through the grass, which was quite long, attempting to get away – those who were not dead. I went forward as I had been told to do, and joined the Adjutant in front of some German anti-tank guns and we began shooting at them. I remember that I owe my life to the quick-wittedness of Captain Cracroft, the Adjutant, because when we got to the potato clamp I found that on the other side of it were half a dozen Germans and so I drove up to them from my side of the potato clamp and gave fire orders to my gunner to fire down into the potato clamp but he couldn't depress the gun far enough. All this time I was standing on the seat of my tank shouting at the gunner and calling to the driver to reverse a bit so that we could get the bullets down low enough, and little did I think that behind me there was a German lying on the ground, with his rifle resting on a pack, drawing a very careful bead on the back of my neck. Well, the Adjutant, I heard later – not till I got back to England – pulled out his revolver and, quick as a flash, he shot the German in the throat. It must have been a jolly good revolver shot, and it saved my life.

An 88mm anti-aircraft gun battery deployed for anti-tank action.

The side of Colonel Fitzmaurice's tank had been blown in and both he and his radio operator, Corporal Moorhouse, had been killed. Major Stuart Fernie, who had survived the debacle, took command of the remainder of the regiment for the rest of the action.

How had all this come to pass? While it was certainly not planned by the Germans as an ambush, the 'killing area' that 4 RTR had driven into had served very well as exactly that. The battalion of 105mm guns on Telegraph Hill, positioned to help screen Arras, had been complemented by their 1st Battalion on the northern side of the ridge between Neuville-Vitasse and Mercatel. Add into the equation a battery of the dual-purpose 88mm guns on the ridge near Mercatel, originally sited to provide anti-aircraft cover to the 7th Panzer's move around Arras, and it is easy to appreciate that the main body of 4 RTR had entered what was, by default, an almost perfect killing area.

On their own, without timely close air, infantry or artillery support to drive the German gunners from their pieces, 4 RTR was extremely vulnerable to an enemy who received very little return fire. Once again it is obvious that all-arms tactics were almost non-existent in the British army of 1940.

This was as far as the 'Arras counter-attack' reached in its attack towards their first objective, the River Cojeul, which was still over 2 miles further on to the east.

The Infantry Arrive

6 DLI, following in the wake of the tanks, arrived on the scene some time after the disaster that had befallen 4 RTR, having made their way through shellfire and the resulting piles of rubble in Achicourt to reach the area of Beaurains. Having crossed the start line it will be recalled that Major Jeffreys had deployed the battalion's four rifle companies: 'I put D Company on the main axis, B Company to the right and C Company to the left and A was back in reserve. We pushed on in artillery formation, with shells coming down harder and harder.'

By the time 6 DLI reached Beaurains, where they had been warned not to advance beyond the village, they saw for themselves the burning wreckage of 4 RTR's attack laid out in front of them. For an infantryman, the columns of smoke rising from what to them were armoured monsters plus the dead and wounded tank crews was a singular shock to men in their first action.

With Colonel Miller back at Main Headquarters 6 DLI, Major Jeffreys was forward with the battalion's small and mobile Advanced Headquarters in order to deploy and control the three leading companies in very difficult circumstances. He explained:

> I had no contact by this time with Battalion Headquarters and the CO. It seemed to me that the only thing we could do was to press on, so we pressed on. We pressed on to a village called Beaurains. When we got to Beaurains I pushed 'C' Company, Ronnie Rodden, up through the village. I said, 'Get to the far end of Beaurains and take up a defensive position there.' 'D' Company I put along the road south, stretching south from Beaurains.
>
> I had a marvellous driver, a chap called Iceton, and I had this 15cwt truck. I said to Iceton, 'Come on, we'll go and try and find "B" Company off to the right' [they had followed C Squadron towards Agny]. So I got in the truck and off we went. I tried to find 'B' Company but couldn't locate them. Trying to find them to the south, I ran into a lot of trouble. Lot of shelling, bit of long distance machine-gun fire, and a good many casualties from 'D' Company who were on this road running south of Beaurains. Iceton and I picked up all the wounded we could, put them in the 15cwt and I said to Iceton, 'Drive back and get all these people into a Regimental Aid Post... Do that and come back to me at the crossroads at Beaurains.'
>
> There I was on my feet by myself. So I walked up to 'C' Company at Beaurains; they were in good heart but extremely tired, as they had all this marching through the previous days, had had little rest, now they'd come up and they'd been marching since this early morning. Fighting a bit, but march, march, march.

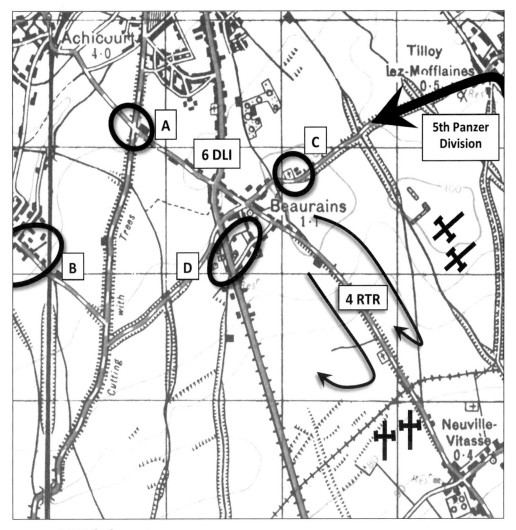

6 DLI deployment.

Major Jeffreys halted C Company on the eastern outskirts of the village, where with leading elements of the 5th Panzer Division in sight less than a mile away around Tilloy-lès-Mofflaines and the enemy artillery in action on Telegraph Hill, they needed no encouragement to take up a hasty defensive position. Securing their area and rounding up prisoners, mainly from the 2nd Battalion, 6th Rifle Regiment, the company started to dig shell scrapes for protection, while the company commander, Major Ronnie Rodden, sited the troop of 2-pounder guns from 151 Brigade Anti-Tank Company to make the defence 'tank-proof'. Major Jeffreys, meanwhile, set off to find D Company who should have been around the crossroads south of Beaurains.

D Company had similarly taken up defensive positions in the southern part of the village and was extended to the south-east along the line of a sunken

A 2-pounder anti-tank gun deployed for action during the Phoney War.

lane. They too had made their approach to Beaurains 'tank-proof' but at this stage the Germans in front of them, other than shelling heavily, were still recovering from the shock eruption of 4 RTR on their flank.

A Company had, meanwhile, on the orders of General Martel been filling in a series of large shell craters and clearing rubble in Achicourt, which was preventing the column's wheeled transport coming forward. A Company also took over most of the 200-odd prisoners that had been rounded up by the forward company.

Behind the infantry, 'Gun Buster' had been belatedly sent forward to act as 368 Battery's Liaison Officer to 6 DLI:

> I jumped into my truck, and accompanied by my wireless operator and driver, started off in the direction of Achicourt, about two miles south of Arras. Our infantry were advancing very rapidly just now. We travelled through country still occupied by small detachments of Germans who had been cut off. Mopping-up parties of Tommies were investigating the farmhouses, and occasionally bringing out a few prisoners. Every now and then a little spasmodic shooting indicated that resistance was still being offered.

Second Lieutenant Tom Allison of C Company a little further ahead in Beaurains was one of those 'mopping up', checking the area allocated to his platoon:

> My platoon went after about fifty Germans hiding in a summer house. They all came out with their hands up. A sergeant and some men

captured another fifty nearby, so in all we had about a hundred prisoners. At this stage some Stukas started to make things unpleasant. It was decided that we had better get the prisoners well to the rear.

I was ordered to take a ten-soldier escort. The prisoners were quite cheerful, certainly in better shape than we were, and some of them said they were Austrians. We gave the prisoners cigarettes, and quite a bit of talk took place between the escort and the prisoners.

At Battalion HQ we were told to take them back to 151 Brigade HQ. This was at a place north of Arras, about two hours' march away. I shared a motorcycle with another man and we rode up and down the column keeping it on the move. The only hint of trouble came when passing through French villages, where civilians shouted insults at the 'Boche'.

368 Battery

Meanwhile, 'Gun Buster' and his liaison party had passed the railway crossing, the start line, which 4 RTR had burst through earlier:

> Everywhere there were signs of fierce shelling and bombing. At a small hamlet just outside Achicourt my truck was held up by a huge crater where a bomb had dropped plumb in the centre of the road. Troops were busy filling in the hole before traffic could pass. The hamlet itself was a heap of ruins... The crater being now filled in, I went forward in my search for the Battalion Headquarters, stopping every now and then to ask an officer or sergeant for information. The answer was always the same: 'Further on.' Evidently the infantry was still going forward. I reached Achicourt, which had suffered heavily from shell-fire, and still there was no sign of the front line. Except for stray parties of troops, and a couple of ambulances into which stretcher parties were loading casualties, the village was deserted.

Leaving Achicourt, the Gunners passed wounded DLI soldiers who were having their injuries dressed by RAMC orderlies. By now it was late afternoon and in the mile of open country between Achicourt and Beaurains there was a mixed bag of British and French tanks scattered along the roadside being repaired by their crews:

> At last, by the cross-roads just outside Beaurains, I found Battalion Headquarters. In a ditch, of all places. A reserve line of infantry was lying in this long shallow ditch for a mile along the roadside, and with them their Colonel and his Second-in-Command.
> 'Good afternoon, sir,' I said, introducing myself. 'I'm gunner liaison officer.'

'Welcome, my boy,' exclaimed the Colonel heartily. 'Take a seat in the ditch. Is your battery ready to fire?'

'Give us a quarter of an hour. What targets would you like us to fire on?'

We scanned our maps for likely enemy concentration points, deciding on four villages along the banks of the River Cojeul, about three miles distant.

'Those villages are our [6 DLI's] final objective,' said the Colonel. 'The enemy will probably try to bring his infantry over the bridges. Anyhow, they're good targets to have a crack at to begin with. Have you any means of communication with your battery?'

Unfortunately, I hadn't. I had followed up the infantry so far that I had exceeded the range of my wireless.

'I'll return to the Battery, give them the targets, send one of the GP officers, and have a telephone line laid direct to you,' I said.

This exchange reveals Colonel Miller's lack of awareness of the situation and potential targets, which were only just beyond the village in front of him, and the lack of communications with the tanks, but above all his tolerance of 368 Battery's plans, or lack of, to communicate from their Battery HQ to Battalion HQ, which was less than 2 miles forward of the start line; a total of about 4 miles. This was, of course, well within the range of the guns and the old gunner adage applies here: 'No comms, no bombs.'

With thirty bombers passing on overhead, 'Gun Buster' had to wait to start his return to the battery, now deploying south of Dainville, a journey that today takes less than twenty minutes:

Near Dainville, about a mile and a half from the area that was to be occupied by our battery position, two French tanks were drawn up stationary on the road alongside a small copse. As I approached, five Messerschmitts wheeled around, one behind the other, in preparation to attack them. The tanks had also seen the planes, and were just closing their turrets. I guessed what was coming their way, and hoped to get past in time to avoid getting a share of it. But I was too late. Just as I came abreast of the tanks the first plane was beginning its dive right overhead. 'Jump for it,' I yelled. I shot out of one side of the truck as my driver and wireless operator took a headlong leap out of the other. I scrambled into a hedgeless ditch by the roadside just as the German machine-guns began to spray the road. My ditch was so shallow that I could only partly conceal my head. Bullets whizzed in front of my face. When they smacked the dry earth at the edge of the ditch puffs of dust spurted up, half blinding me. Every now and then a bullet flew so close that the blast hit me in the face like a punch, and I touched myself to see if I had been wounded, and was quite surprised not to find blood on my hand. For nearly ten minutes the fight went on, the planes circling around a hundred feet up and the tanks firing back at them. When silence came I poked my head up gingerly out of the ditch.

'Gun Buster's' bullet-riddled vehicle excited much interest when he arrived at the gun position that was just being laid out by the Gun Position Officer (GPO):

'I've got some targets,' I said to the Major, and explained the infantry's need of us. 'Harassing fire tasks.' And the Command Post Officer settled down to work them out from my map.

Boyd, M-Troop commander, whom the Major had selected as the forward OP [Observation Post] officer, came up to me before leaving for a chat about possibilities.

'Our forward line is in front of Beaurains,' I said, 'and I don't think you'll do better for an OP than the village church. You should get a pretty view from the belfry.'

'I love sightseeing,' he said with a grin, and hurried off with his OP Ack, telephonist and wireless operator. Behind followed a cable-laying truck with half a dozen signallers, and the NCO in charge on a motor-cycle.

Even though the gun positions had already been marked out and target data was being worked on, the guns had yet to arrive from their hide back at Anzin-St. Aubin. 'Gun Buster' continued:

Suddenly, as we stood looking down the road, a mass of bombers roared above and began to bomb Dainville (which was already under shell fire) and its surroundings. The thunder of the explosions was terrific. Huge clouds of smoke and dust swirled in the air, a score of fires were started, and the whole village was blotted out from our view by a solid pall, behind which it didn't take much imagination to guess the horrors that were happening.

And at this very moment, where on the far side the road curved down to the village, we saw the long line of Y [368] Battery vehicles driving straight into this inferno. A battery going into action stops for nothing. Before we had time to gasp they had disappeared, swallowed up in the deadly chaos that was going on behind that dark curtain.

At this point, out in the open the Battery HQ and Gun Position party were spotted by a squadron of nine Stukas:

We saw them coming at us in flights of three. They circled around overhead and on the second circle formed in line to make their dive…

Ju 87 Stukas.

straight at us, with a nerve-shattering scream that rose to a crescendo the nearer they came. At about five hundred feet from the ground, three bombs, like a clutch of black ostrich eggs, dropped from the plane. They also seemed to be coming straight for us.

A wild rush for cover resulted, but once the bombs had fallen and the Stukas had departed the only damage was a punctured tyre on one of the trucks:

Glancing up the road, to our joy and amazement we beheld the leading gun-tractor of 368 Battery just emerging from the smoke and conflagration and tumult of Dainville. And behind it another tractor. And another.

We stood there counting them aloud as they rumbled out of that dreadful holocaust in which we had feared they were lost forever.

Meanwhile, Lieutenant Boyd had duly established his OP in the Beaurains church tower and indeed had a good view but the battery's radio net was indifferent and his telephone cable repeatedly cut. As a result, with the battery now in action for most of the time they were, less than fully usefully, firing on the crossings of the River Cojeul, which was to have been the first objective but the advance would never get anywhere near it. Not only that, but 368 Battery was firing off the map, without corrections to the fall of shot and therefore it was not very accurate.

The Battle Around Agny

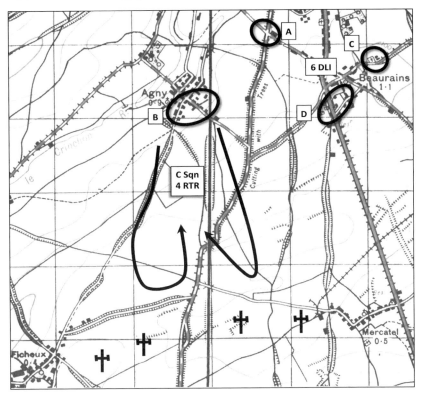

C Squadron and B Company at Agny.

C Squadron of 4 RTR, instead of following the swing of the battalion to the left around Arras as planned, had been ordered to cover the right rear of the main advance, which should have been covered by 7 RTR but they had, as we have seen, been delayed by getting off route. Consequently, C Squadron swept down on the village of Agny, with B Company, 6 DLI being tasked to follow them.

With the infantry well over a mile behind, C Squadron's Mk I and Matilda tanks continued to advance on their own towards the Mercatel-Ficheux Ridge. Here by 1520 hours [BEF time] the Germans had established another but very much ad hoc anti-tank screen with some 105mm guns and anti-tank guns from the *SS Totenkopf*, who had continued to move up on the 7th Panzer's left during the previous hour. Together these guns halted C Squadron's advance up the ridge at the outskirts of Mercatel with the loss of several tanks. The fire was intense but as they withdrew in a westerly sweep they overran some *SS Totenkopf* anti-tank guns and dispersed the frightened gunners.

Krupp Protze towing a 37mm gun crewed by the SS Totenkopf.

Despite the general ineffectiveness of the German anti-tank fire, it was a combination of the 88s firing from the squadron's left and a battery of 105mm artillery pieces that halted the advance of C Squadron and, in the process, knocked out more than a few tanks.

Meanwhile, B Company, 6 DLI had arrived and had cleared Agny, adding to the haul of prisoners in the process. They too were quickly dug in with anti-tank guns on the southern side of the village and in the sunken lanes.

An example of the fluidity of the situation is the experience of Sergeant Strickland aboard his Mk I tank who, returning to a point near the village of Écurie to the north of Arras for replenishment of ammunition and repairs to his tank, encountered enemy infantry. He drove them into what proved to be a cul-de-sac, where they took cover in a barn. He put several bursts of machine-gun fire through the door and demanded loudly that they come out. To his surprise up to fifty fully-armed German infantrymen threw down their weapons and surrendered to him, little knowing that Strickland was now out of ammunition. With only his driver, this presented the same problem as earlier but a single DLI straggler helped to keep the prisoners in order by mounting the tank and waving his rifle menacingly at them.

Chapter 8

The Right Column's Battle

With 4 RTR already in action, 7 RTR was still moving forward thanks to its deviation from its route from the assembly area at Marœuil to the start line at the railway. Lieutenant Tom Craig, clearly still too far to the left, recalled:

> Before crossing the railway, we came across isolated groups of our own infantry – DLI and not the ones we were supposed to work with [6th rather than 8th] – and also saw, and had, a half-hearted battle with what turned out to be French tanks sitting in the open on the high ground 1,000 yards west of Achicourt [most likely between Dainville and Achicourt].

This half-hearted battle resulted in four French tanks being knocked out before the error was realized and stopped by a squadron commander standing up, waving his arms and shouting amidst the din of battle: '*Je suis Anglais* – fucking stop firing':

> Once the mistake was realised we moved on into the village and met up with some of the 4th, B Squadron of the 7th and Scout Cars of the GHQ Recce Unit (one commanded by Lt Newton Dunn) [12th Lancers]. They had knocked out a German anti-tank gun, and taken a few prisoners on the southern outskirts on the road to Wailly.

Eventually some order was restored within the scattered ranks of 7 RTR, with A Squadron on the left following the line of the northerly railway spur and then south-east towards Mercatel. This is, however, where C Squadron of 4 RTR, in the earlier absence of 7 RTR, was already in action around Agny, covering the right rear of the rest of their own regiment. The remainder of 7 RTR attempted to regain its correct alignment by following the general line of the pylons to the south-west before turning south onto the correct axis. In the centre, D Squadron was directed toward Ficheux, while B Squadron on the right was heading towards Wailly.

Among those who were too far to the east was Sergeant Heppel, mounted in a light tank arriving at the railway line, who also found 'the level-crossing

Hotchkiss H35 light tank.

near Dainville closed, so I was compelled to break through it, and proceeded about half a mile at high speed'. C Squadron and some of the rear of the battalion also crossed via the level crossing.

From the outset 7 RTR had been dispersed by coming off route and consequently went into action as troops and in some cases as individual tanks. Lieutenant Craig's experience is illustrative. After a brief halt at Achicourt he was ordered to move west and on to Wailly and took over the lead from A Squadron HQ. He recalled:

> I was entirely on my own as the other tank troops had not caught up. About 500 yards from the village I was fired on by a large armoured car with a small gun in it; 20mm I suppose, with no effect on my tank. I fired back and the car burst into flames. One of the crew must have had guts, as although wounded he continued to fire as I closed in and eventually I saw him climb out and fall into the gutter, badly burned. I moved past the blazing armoured car nearly up to the cross-roads in the village which was full of German infantry. There was a lot of traffic darting across the crossroads from south to north, which we engaged with varying success.

Meanwhile, Major King and Sergeant Doyle in their Matilda spotted and engaged two troops of enemy anti-tank guns, knocked out a pair of armoured cars, the latter probably from the 37th Reconnaissance Battalion, and then stalked and destroyed an 88mm gun.

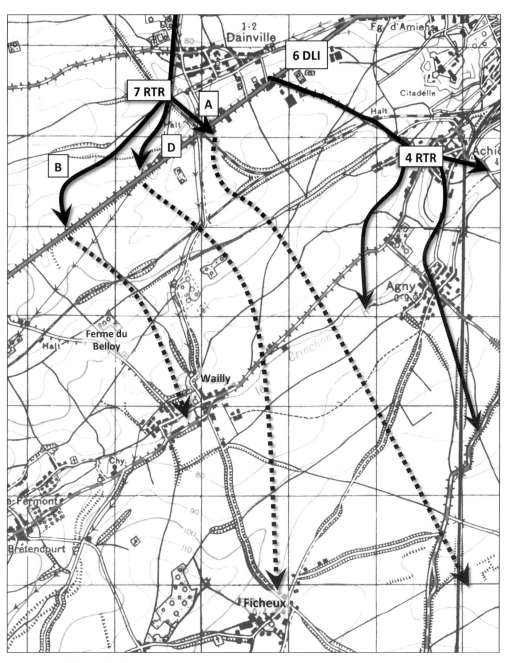

7 RTR Right Column.

Sd.Kfz 222 armoured car.

A Flak 36 88mm gun, 1940.

Pak 36 37mm anti-tank gun ready for action during the 1940 campaign.

Two Matildas approach the German 88mm gun line on the D34 west of Mercatel. The tank commanders are believed to be Major King and Sergeant Doyle and they clearly have the German gun crew under fire.

Sergeant Heppel who had earlier burst through the level crossing gates in his light tank was still pushing on south over the ridge and down into the valley of the River Crinchon between Wailly and Agny:

> I then followed two Mk II tanks of 6 Section B Squadron intending to pass them and catch up with the Mk I vehicles.
> Odd groups of the enemy were seen and engaged, but near a main road [the Wailly road that the 6th Rifle Regiment had been using] west of Achicourt we came under anti-tank fire and sustained three direct hits. The effect was that of hitting a large stone at speed, and the track on the right-hand side was seen a yard or two in front of the tank. Two more shots followed, and then the guns were silenced by our fire, and that of the Mark I tanks, which went on without seeing what had happened to

A Mark I tank of the type commanded by Sergeant Heppel.

It is clear from German situation maps that A Squadron had run into the head of the 2nd Battalion, 6th Rifle Regiment. A concentration of anti-tank guns west of Agny and beyond had only managed a mobility kill of Sergeant Heppel's light tank before themselves being overrun and dispersed. However, Sergeant Heppel was able to witness first-hand the effect of a lack of infantry to mop up and secure ground taken by the tanks:

> We were subjected to intense rifle fire for some minutes, and then left alone, apparently in the belief that we were all killed. After five or ten minutes about thirty to fifty Germans were congregated in groups on the road and to the right of us. We estimated the range of each group, and then opened fire. Many of the enemy fell, but some doubtless were unhurt. Later an abandoned anti-tank gun, about 800 yards to our right front, was re-manned, but was again seen to be deserted after we fired upon it.

Elsewhere, with the departure of the tanks and with no infantry having yet arrived in the area, in many cases the Germans started to recover their balance.

Rommel
As 7 RTR's attack had got under way, Rommel was with his command party in his accustomed position towards the front of the 25th Panzer Regiment who

88mm gun, Sd.Kfz. 7 half-track and range-finder party, France 1940.

had reached the Scarpe, and retraced his route back south to 'chase up' the 7th Rifle Regiment who were lagging behind but they were nowhere to be found. He later wrote:

> A mile or so north of Ficheux we eventually came across part of the 6th Rifle Regiment, and driving alongside their column, turned off with them towards Wailly. Half a mile east of the village we came under fire from the north. One of our howitzer batteries was already in position at the northern exit from the village, firing rapidly on enemy tanks attacking southward from Arras.

It would seem that this part of the 6th Rifle Regiment and Rommel himself were unaware of the action just over a mile away to the north-east. The noise of open vehicles and the fact that in 1940, no matter how good German communicators were, commanders could rarely communicate effectively once on the move, which probably accounts for this. Rommel continued:

> As we were now coming under machine-gun fire and the infantry had already taken cover to the right, Lieutenant Most and I ran on in front of the armoured cars towards a battery position. It did not look as though the battery would have much difficulty in dealing with the enemy tanks [A Squadron, 7 RTR], for the gunners were calmly hurling round after round into them in complete disregard of the return fire. Running along behind the battery lines, we arrived at Wailly and then called up the vehicles. The enemy tank fire had created chaos and confusion among our troops in the village and they were jamming up the roads and yards with their vehicles, instead of going into action with every available weapon to fight off the oncoming enemy.

Rommel was forward with the 25th Panzer Regiment and its commander Oberst *Rithenberg on the River Scarpe at the time of the British attack. A command variant of the Panzer II is in the background.*

Rommel on the move in a Kfz.15 car with a command variant Sd.Kfz. 232 tactical headquarters armoured car as escort.

Rommel had come under fire from some 4 RTR tanks that had followed the Crinchon Valley and penetrated between the villages of Wailly and Ficheux. From the profusion of bold red lines on Rommel's situation map towards Mercatel and up the Crinchon Valley, one could conclude that this was a major penetration of the German positions. It was, however, nothing of the sort and is an example of how a mere handful of tanks involved in this action had caused panic. Eventually the lonely tanks deep in enemy territory turned around in the valley south of Brétencourt, having encountered elements of the *SS Totenkopf* who had also been put into a state of panic. The *SS Totenkopf*'s 3rd SS Infantry Regiment, however, once they too had recovered from the shock of 7 RTR erupting into their flank, played their part in halting and turning back the penetration that went well beyond Wailly.

SS Totenkopf in the act of deploying. Note the Swastika air recognition flag on the engine deck of the Sd.Kfz. 221 armoured car.

Colonel Hector Heyland and his adjutant were forward directing the attack on Wailly, but without radio communication they had to dismount from their tanks to give orders and in doing so both were killed by machine-gun fire.

Lieutenant Craig was in one of the A Squadron tanks closing in on Wailly and continued to engage German transport:

> When occupied with this all of a sudden, they tried to push a little 37mm anti-tank gun round the corner to fire at me at short range, again with no effect and we drove them back. I got closer to the village near to a garden wall and a shower of grenades were thrown over the wall onto my tank.
>
> I now felt that as I was alone in the village and vulnerable to this sort of attack, I should withdraw, and this I did into the field to the north of the burning armoured cars. I stayed there until a light tank from the recce troop told me to come back to Achicourt.

See map on page 113.

While the fighting between Agny and Ficheux was going on, D Squadron's attack south towards Wailly was under way, with the unsupported tanks advancing across the Doullens road and railway line. Rommel, meanwhile, in his own words, having seen the confusion that his men had fallen into as the attack began tried to create order.

> After notifying the divisional staff of the RTR's critical situation in and around Wailly we drove off to a hill 1,000 metres [north] west of the village [Ferme du Belloy], where we found a light anti-aircraft platoon and several anti-tank guns located in hollows and a small wood, most of them totally under cover. About 1,200 metres west of our position [in fact much closer than that], the leading enemy tanks, among them one heavy, had already crossed the Arras-Beaumetz railway and shot up one of our Panzers. At the same time several enemy tanks were advancing… across the railway line towards Wailly. It was an extremely tight spot, for there were also several enemy tanks very close to Wailly on its northern side. The crew of a howitzer battery, some distance away, now left their guns, swept along by the retreating infantry. With [Lieutenant] Most's help, I brought every available gun into action at top speed against the tanks. Every gun, both anti-tank and anti-aircraft, was ordered to open rapid fire immediately and I personally gave each gun its target. With the enemy tanks so perilously close, only rapid fire from every gun could save the situation. We ran from gun to gun. The objections of gun commanders that the range was still too great to engage the tanks effectively were overruled. All I cared about was to halt the enemy tanks by heavy gunfire. Soon we succeeded in putting the leading enemy tanks out of action. About 150 yards west of our small

Rommel observes, France 1940, possibly accompanied by Leutnant Most.

wood a British captain climbed out of a heavy tank and walked unsteadily towards us with his hands up. We had killed his driver. Over by the howitzer battery also – despite a range of 1,200 to 5,500 metres – the rapid fire of our anti-tank and anti-aircraft guns succeeded in bringing the enemy to a halt and forcing some of them to turn away.

This deluge of fire is exactly the doctrine that Rommel espoused for use in a tight spot in his book *Infantry Attacks*, written between the wars, and used so effectively when crossing the River Meuse a week earlier with the French on the high ground beyond. It was designed to have a psychological effect on the enemy. Rommel continued:

We now directed our fire against the other group of tanks attacking from the direction of Bac du Nord, and succeeded in keeping the tanks off, setting fire to some, halting others and forcing the rest to retreat. Although we were under very heavy fire from the tanks during this action, the gun crews worked magnificently. The worst seemed to be over and the attack beaten off, when suddenly [Lieutenant] Most sank to the ground behind a 20mm anti-aircraft gun close beside me. He was mortally wounded and blood gushed from his mouth. I had had no idea that there was any firing in our vicinity at that moment, apart from that of the 20mm gun. Now however, the enemy suddenly started dropping

Matilda Mark II tank.

heavy gunfire into our position in the wood. Poor Most was beyond help and died before he could be carried into cover beside the gun position. The death of this brave man, a magnificent soldier, touched me deeply.

Rommel's personal intervention and leadership in the battle on the ridge at Ferme du Belloy had been instrumental in steadying his men and applying that deluge of fire that had brought 7 RTR, D Squadron in particular, to a halt.

8 DLI
With 7 RTR in action to their front and B and C companies covering their rear in Duisans, A Company, followed by D Company, Battalion HQ and a scout

platoon were, as Major English explained, by 1700 hours working their way through Warlus

> … searching the farms and the houses and had reached the south side of the village at about 5.30. They then went down to Bernouville, which they cleared and then came out on this side moving towards the Arras-Doullens road. When they got about 200–300 yards to the south of Bernouville they came under extremely heavy fire from light automatics, machine guns and indeed mortars.
>
> D Company was moving up behind the Advance Guard, they were directed by the CO into the eastern edge of Warlus and the forward edge of the wood to the south of the village. They took about a dozen German prisoners.
>
> Soon after we got into Warlus we were subjected to a Stuka attack by about twenty planes. They came over and dived down. They had a mechanism so that when they dived they made a tremendous shrieking noise and it seemed they were aiming their bombs directly at you. We all flattened ourselves into the earth.

See map on following page.

Hitherto, even though enemy aircraft had been seen overhead throughout the day the *Luftwaffe* had confined themselves to planned sorties on Arras and the immediate surrounding area where 368 Battery had earlier felt their lash, but all that was to change and virtually any movement by tanks or infantry henceforth came under attack by the *Luftwaffe* in the wider battle area:

Stuka pilots being briefed for a sortie.

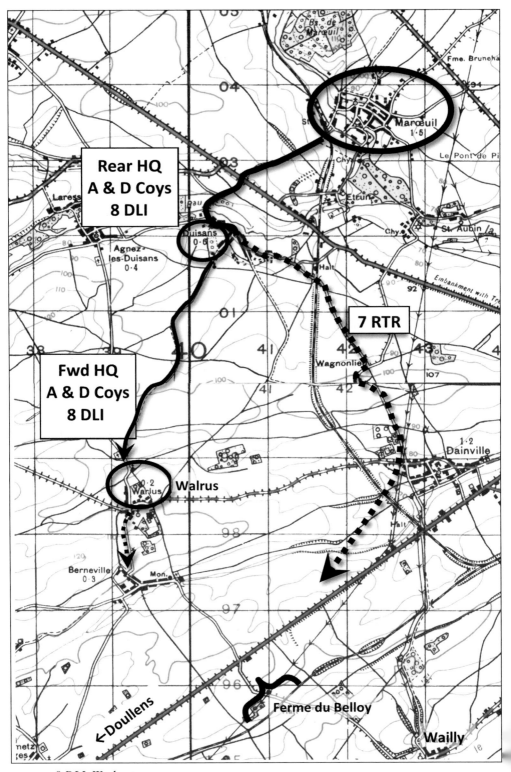

Rear HQ
A & D Coys
8 DLI

7 RTR

Fwd HQ
A & D Coys
8 DLI

Walrus

Ferme du Belloy

←Doullens

Wailly

8 DLI, Warlus area.

We were over on the left between the woods and the water-tower and trying to get the chaps into positions and we were caught in the open. The attack went on for about ten to fifteen minutes and each plane seemed to drop five or six bombs, one at a time. There was quite a bit of our transport on the road around the water-tower. The attack was almost unopposed, and we had an Ack-Ack platoon with HQ Company and they had one truck with Bren guns mounted on tripods and a gunner was firing from this truck until the truck just in front of him was hit. He then took cover. The actual damage was slight. They damaged three trucks and about ten men were wounded in the two forward companies and Battalion HQ, but the morale damage was very considerable. It was the first time we had been in action and we were subjected to this terrifying aerial attack and everyone was absolutely shattered. After a few minutes the officers and some of the NCOs collected themselves and said 'Right, we must get on with it', but it was very difficult to get some of the men moving – we had to kick them into position and the effect was very considerable. As the campaign went on we were frequently dive-bombed and by the second time and certainly by the third time the chaps realised that the bark of the Stuka was very much worse than its actual bite, and we began to take very little notice of them – casualties were caused, but the morale effect had gone.

This air attack was the result of an emergency request for close air support by HQ 7th Panzer Division and was only a foretaste of what was to come.

Rommel, having stabilized the situation, now set about turning the tables on the British and later wrote:

While this heavy fighting had been going on around the 6th and 7th Rifle Regiments, Rothenburg's 25th Panzer Regiment had reached its objective in a dashing advance, and then waited in vain for the arrival of the Reconnaissance Battalion and the Rifle Regiments. At about 1900 hours [1800 hours BEF time] I gave orders for the Panzer Regiment to thrust south-eastwards in order to take the enemy armour advancing south from Arras in the flank and rear. During this operation, the Panzer Regiment clashed with a superior force of heavy and light enemy tanks and many guns south of Agnez. Fierce fighting flared up, tank against tank, an extremely heavy engagement in which the Panzer Regiment destroyed seven heavy tanks and six anti-tank guns and broke through the enemy position.

The 'superior force' was, of course, by then only scattered French units and the remnants of the two RTR battalions and anti-tank guns of 151 Brigade, so is something of an exaggeration.

To return to 8 DLI in Warlus, they were by early evening running low on ammunition and coming under pressure from the south of Bernouville, with both the company commander and the company sergeant major being wounded and taken prisoner by German infantry, who had by now well and truly recovered from their earlier panic. Major England continued his account of the battle:

> From the woods at Warlus we saw German tanks approaching and they came up a re-entrant and got to within 150 yards of us. The French Interpreter grabbed a Bren gun and ran down the road and got this gun into action. He shot up the tanks and some infantry who were with them – possibly tank crews who had got out but anyway there were men on the ground. This must have had some effect because the Germans withdrew. For that action [the French Sergeant] was awarded the DCM. The CO was wounded with a wound in the top of his leg but we didn't notice much difference. He just went around limping and carried on directing the battle.

Somua S35 tank.

Several French tanks had at some point in the late afternoon joined the DLI in Warlus and when they came out of their covered positions and engaged, the German panzers, who were by now returning in strength, withdrew:

Now we came under heavier and heavier fire from the ridge as well as from artillery and this was causing quite a few casualties. OC D Company was now wounded, as was one of the platoon commanders; both were subsequently taken prisoner a few hours later. Another platoon commander was missing and the village was gradually becoming a shambles, with the enemy's fire setting light to the thatched houses and as it grew dark the place became like Blackpool.

As the attacks mounted the CO pulled back A Company and withdrew the perimeter a little bit to make a tighter all-round defence; unfortunately, we still had no artillery support. The French tanks that had been with us said they had to leave – they had something else to do, but they said they would be back after dark but we rather doubted that they would return.

Our communications with the rest of the Battalion were causing a problem. B and C Companies, under the Battalion Second-in-Command, were still back in Duisans. The idea had been to bring them up when we had made Warlus firm. Two or three dispatch riders were sent back to Duisans but they couldn't get through. German tanks were by now moving across the track between the two villages and there didn't appear to be a way of reporting our situation to Brigade HQ.

Across the battlefield south of Arras, the situation which had for a short while in the early afternoon been favourable for Frankforce had been stabilized by Rommel and the Germans were now clearly in the ascendancy. Without a cohesive command structure or communications across the two brigades, it was more a question of saving what they could of the tanks and infantry rather than holding on to gains.

Chapter 9

The Withdrawal

It wasn't so much a decision for the elements of Frankforce south and south-west of Arras to pull back, more that they were being forced back from Beaurains, Agny and Achicourt and isolated in Warlus. General Martel, along with brigadiers Pratt and Churchill, was bowing to the inevitable and struggling to round up and save as many of their scattered forces as they could.

At around 2000 hours the two brigadiers formally ordered a withdrawal: the right column to positions north of le Gy Rau at Marœuil and the left to the railway line between Achicourt and Dainville, i.e. the former start line.

The Left Column
Only gradually, though, did the fighting ebb away. Lieutenant Peter Vaux in his Mk VI Light Tank was out to exact revenge on the 105mm artillery battery on Telegraph Hill that had virtually wiped out A and D squadrons:

> We then turned our machine guns on the woods, and we just sprayed the trees. To our astonishment all sorts of Germans and bits of equipment and things fell down out of the trees, where I suppose they had taken refuge.
>
> … the fire became heavier and heavier and there were shells falling all round us and striking the tanks, including the tanks already knocked out, and it was high time for us to go, and the Adjutant signalled to me to turn around and drive back. …As we drove back through the Matildas my heart sank because I realised what had happened: there were all those tanks that I knew so well – the familiar names – Dreadnought, Dauntless, Demon, Devil; there were the faces of these men with whom I had played games, swum, lived with for years – lying there dead; and there were these tanks – useless, very few of them burning, but most of them smashed up in one way or another. As the Adjutant and I drove back up to the top of the hill, I realised that this really was it. This was tragedy, this was the end of the 4th Tanks as we knew it. In that valley, the best of crews, our tanks, our soldiers, our officers were left behind.

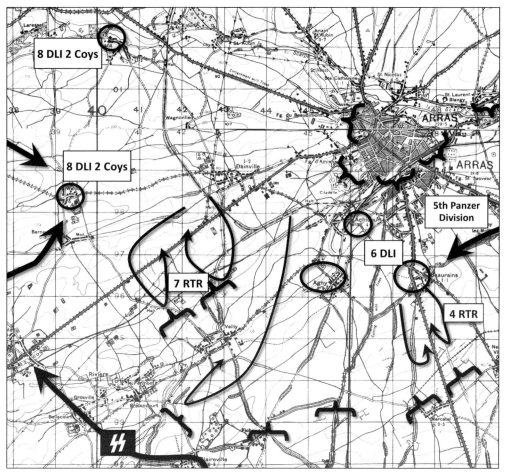

8 DLI 2 Coys

8 DLI 2 Coys

5th Panzer Division

6 DLI

7 RTR

4 RTR

The situation at dusk.

Brigadier Pratt, however, with the wreckage of 4 RTR smouldering in the fields between Beaurains and Neuville-Vitesse, was among the first of the senior officers to realize that the operation was effectively over:

> By about 6.30 p.m. it was evident that without proper support we were not going to make the River Sensée. The infantry were exhausted, both from sheer fatigue and from shelling and air attacks. The Boche tanks had previously gone the wrong way, but by this time the first panic was dying down and he was pulling himself together. A halt was called and our tanks rallied just behind the few handfuls of infantry on the ground.

Sergeant Heppel of D Squadron, 4 RTR, who had earlier suffered a mobility kill, was still trying to repair his light tank:

> … there was a hole about two inches in diameter in the right-hand sprocket which had two teeth missing, and the radiator, which could not

Repairs to a Mark I in a French village in 1940.

be opened, was leaking. The engine would run, but smelt strongly of burning. I made several attempts to get more track plates while my crew, Troopers Tansley and Mackay M, worked at the tank often under fairly heavy shell fire. At times this was so severe that work had to be suspended. Enemy aircraft also caused interference.

Back in the area of Marœuil 9 DLI had a grandstand view of the *Luftwaffe* in action above Sergeant Heppel and the rest of the forward battalions:

It was so terrific as to suggest they were showing off and was rather like the air attack in H.G. Wells's film *Things to Come* only more so. They put in 200-300 planes of all sorts and kept it up for an hour and a half while we walked slowly along the road. They were dropping salvoes of heavy and lighter stuff. The crescendo of sound was extraordinary and continuous with detonations and the scream of dive-bombers. The attack, of course, was mainly on the two battalions in front, who had a hell of a time as they were almost simultaneously counter-attacked by heavy tanks and the attack was brought to a standstill.

Private Bert Davies of 6 LI recalled the Stuka raid: 'You felt so helpless. You haven't enough strength to retaliate. As long as you can retaliate a bit you feel all right…you lie down and take it. It was pretty disheartening. You feel as if you've got no protection whatsoever.'

As already noted that this was the only time the Stukas gained the moral ascendancy over the Durhams and they soon learned that their bark was worse than their bite, taking many bombs to actually do much damage.

These German air attacks continued until dusk was falling and illustrates the use of aircraft as a key part of the blitzkrieg, summoned up by radio to deliver crushing blows. However, as the sky above the Arras battlefield darkened, the enemy aircraft finally departed. Sergeant Heppel continued his report:

> At dusk, most of the infantry had withdrawn and since it was obvious that a counter-attack was coming and that in the dark I could do no useful work against it I prepared to abandon the tank. I set fire to three German motor-cycles (one a combination from which I removed a map, later given to Captain Holden) and the three anti-tank guns. These were nearly all metal so did not burn well. They appeared similar to a very large Boys rifle in mechanism, firing a shell of about 3☐ to 1lb judging from the empty cases.
>
> All movable kit, including guns, wireless, pyrenes, etc., was piled on an abandoned Bren carrier which we managed to start, and when it was obvious no help was coming, the tank was fired. It was soon blazing fiercely.
>
> Being informed that Neuville-Vitasse was in enemy hands I rallied with Major Fernie of the 4th Bn outside Achicourt.

As darkness fell, the pace of Rommel's operations did not slacken. At 2015 hours, it was reported that German motor-cycle troops and infantry were pushing forward strongly and were in danger of outflanking B Company, 6 DLI in Agny to the west. If they made much more progress and reached Achicourt, the enemy could cut the battalion off from its line of withdrawal to Dainville. Therefore it was not a moment too soon that Colonel Miller received the order to withdraw. Without radio communications to his second-in-command Major

Ground crew prepare a Stuka for its next sortie.

Not mentioned in any account but the 7th Panzer Division had 705 Battery consisting of six self-propelled 150mm Sig 33 infantry guns mounted on a Panzer 1 chassis.

Jeffreys, who was forward with the companies at Beaurains and Agny, this would be easier said than done. The task fell to the Adjutant Captain Ferens and his motorcycle:

> It was quite exciting on a motor bike getting up to the forward companies, because I had no idea whether there were still snipers about. You just had to take your chance and go. I went and did what the CO asked me to do and went up to the forward companies…to tell the company commanders to withdraw, to consolidate back on the Scarpe because we had come up against an absolute solid wall.

Major Jeffreys received the message at 2030 hours and immediately set out to pass the message to C and D companies in Beaurains, who were the most exposed to the impact of the latest German movements:

I had no communication. I had nobody with me. So I went up to Ronnie [Major Rodden of C Company] at the east end of Beaurains and I said, 'You must withdraw.' ...He said, 'Well, I'll try.' I went back to the other end of Beaurains to D Company and when I got there a runner came back from Ronnie saying that there were enemy tanks working round both flanks and he would try and gradually withdraw. There was nothing else he could do... By this time darkness had started to fall.

These were a handful of tanks from 5th Panzer Division, which had also been rushed forward and were advancing on Beaurains from Tilloy-lès-Mofflaines from the east. Meanwhile, 25th Panzer Regiment had been ordered to retrace its route from the Scarpe, some 10 miles from Agny and Beaurains but were tangling with what Rommel reported as 'a superior armoured force at Agnez-lès-Duisans' and were delayed. These were French tanks from the 3rd DLM, in action astride le Gy Rau and in a running action as far south as Duisans. They prevented the panzers from coming into action in the last of the daylight and overwhelming the by now much-reduced and fragmented British. Even so it was touch and go for Major Jeffreys in the darkness that now enveloped the battlefield:

...the Intelligence Officer [the Adjutant Captain Ferens] of the 4th Tanks came along on a motor bike. I said we were going to withdraw to Achicourt... At this moment we heard some tanks coming down the road from C Company on the other side of Beaurains towards us. I said to this chap, 'Whose tanks are these? Yours?' We could see them up the road after a bit, about two hundred yards away. 'Yes,' he said, 'that's alright. They're our Matildas.' The leading tank came on to the crossroad. This tank man and I walked up to the leading tank and in the gloom at about ten paces, I looked straight at the man with his head out of the top of the tank and he was a German. He had these things on his collar. Then he realised that I was an Englishman so he shut the top of his tank like hell and I ran across the front of his tank, for I realised what was going to happen was that he was going to open up on us. But I thought that the thing to do was to get down in front of his tank so he couldn't depress his guns at me. I nipped across the front of the tank and got into the ditch on the far side of him. There were a couple more tanks behind him and they opened up...but behind us were two or three of our own tanks and they engaged the German tanks.

This mutual night engagement 'resolved itself into a noisy, un-lethal firework display' that ruined the already limited night vision of both sets of tanks, who withdrew from this close-quarter engagement. The Durhams were not so lucky! Withdrawing across the open ground towards Achicourt with illuminating flares arcing up above them, they suffered casualties particularly from the panzers' machine guns. The Durhams had the presence of mind to return the fire, hoping to hit the tank commanders' heads, which were out of their hatches. Closed down at night, the Germans would have been virtually blind as to what was going on outside their panzers and even if the return fire didn't hit them, the crack of a .303 bullet overhead would be enough for a tank commander to know that someone was trying to kill him!

C Company on the eastern side of Beaurains had the most difficult task, with the company commander, Major Rodden, covering the withdrawal of his platoons. Having escaped, he and several others from company headquarters were not so lucky when they too mistook German armour for French and were duly taken prisoner by elements of a German Panzer Reconnaissance battalion. 'Gun Buster' of 386 Battery in his liaison role returned to Achicourt and 6 DLI, looking for Colonel Miller but not expecting to find him:

> But the Colonel was still in the ditch at the cross-roads. The change that had taken place in the situation was not the one I expected. Shadowy figures of men, in ones, twos and threes, were moving over the darkening fields towards us. They ran forward, crouching as they came. In the gloom I took them for Germans, and a thrill ran through me at stepping right into the middle of an attack. At any moment I expected to hear the crackle of our infantry fire from the waiting troops in the ditch. I crouched down by the Colonel in the ditch.
>
> 'Germans?' I asked, trying to speak coolly.
>
> 'No, damn it,' he replied. 'That's our front line coming back. We've withdrawn from Beaurains.'

In the confusion of a withdrawal in contact the DLI had forgotten to tell the gunners grouped with their column or their forward observation officer (FOO) up in the Beaurains church tower that they were going back. 'Gun Buster' only had a short time in which to react:

> 'Drive like hell to Beaurains,' I told the driver, looking to see that my revolver was loaded. We covered the distance, about a thousand yards, in no time. The shell-marked village was deadly silent. Not a sound in the streets, not a soul to be seen, British or German. Its unnatural hush and utter emptiness produced a queer effect in the deepening twilight. Much too quiet to be good. Swinging round a corner on two wheels, I came across our cable party busily engaged laying the wire back to the Battery, and utterly oblivious of their peril.
>
> 'Cut the wire and get back to the cross roads,' I yelled, without stopping.
>
> Boyd's truck was standing outside the church. 'Get that engine running at once,' I shouted to his driver, and dashed into the building.

A knocked-out 2-pounder and other vehicles.

'Gun Buster', his driver and the FOO raced out of the village back to Achicourt as a German 'success' Very light arced up into the sky.

The Right Column's Withdrawal

In the early evening 9 DLI had been brought forward to Marœuil alongside Brigade HQ and put on notice to move with a view to being available to cover the withdrawal of the two tank battalions and their fellow Durhams, if necessary. Colonel Percy wrote:

> On first arrival in the village, which was a big one, it was possible to dispose of our mass of transport under cover but after the arrival of the [logistic tail of] 8 DLI, another battery of anti-tank guns and some more of the Northumberland Fusiliers, it was impossible to put away any of their vehicles under cover and the streets of the village were crammed with transport. Incidentally, in the village when we arrived, was a petrol point, consisting of a number of large lorries carrying several thousand gallons of petrol and an ammunition point with many tons of shells and high explosives. The prospects for the next morning were thus not very rosy if the Boche had elected to turn on the sort of air attack we had seen during the evening.

Meanwhile, forward at Bernaville and Warlus, the two companies of 8 DLI were suffering mounting casualties and had been forced to withdraw from Bernaville and were consolidating in Warlus under mounting pressure. Major English recalled that: 'It was getting dark and casualties were increasing. The CO reorganized the perimeter and withdrew a little bit more. We were approached by German Infantry ... We returned fire with our Brens and rifles and the attacks were not pressed.'

With the situation continuing to deteriorate, eventually Second Lieutenant Potts, the mortar platoon commander, was instructed to withdraw through the enemy, who were by now to all intents surrounding the battalion, back to

Brigade HQ at Marœuil. In the event the withdrawal consisted of a hair-raising, breakneck ride on a motor-cycle through the German screen around Warlus, with bullets and tracer rounds cracking around the young officer.

Arriving at 2330 hours and reporting to Brigadier Churchill, he passed on Colonel Beart's message and described the 8th Battalion's situation in Warlus and Duisans. Potts, in a scarcely less dramatic ride, made it back to Duisans with the message to withdraw. He was, however, unable to reach Colonel Beart along with A and D companies at Warlus. Consequently, B and C companies in Duisans under Major McLaren, the battalion's second-in-command, had to withdraw on their own:

> The order then came from Brigade to withdraw back to Marœuil and Vimy. B and C Coys (at Duisans) set off on foot over the fields and reached Vimy in due course at about first light. Because they were marching there was a problem with evacuating the wounded who were too bad to be moved. The doctor decided to stay with them in the RAP in the Château at Duisans.

The withdrawal from Duisans was the easy part of the operation. It was only a couple of miles from Marœuil and 9 DLI had been ordered to assist by sending elements of Z Company, 4 RNF, the battalion's carriers and some anti-tank guns forward. Two friendly forces – one mounted on unfamiliar-sounding armour – at night and in the midst of a battle would normally be a recipe for friendly fire but the Fusiliers, Durhams and Gunners, no doubt fearful as well as being in their first action, showed admirable fire discipline.

Major McLaren's group arrived in Marœuil at 0100 hours on 22 May. Of the commanding officer and the companies at Warlus nothing was heard, but with an increasing number of reports from 9 DLI's patrols of growing enemy activity, fears grew that they had been destroyed.

Forward at Warlus A and D companies were, however, still isolated and surrounded. Not only that, they were much reduced in numbers and running very low on ammunition; their destruction or surrender beckoned. However, soon after midnight, unexpectedly, as earlier promised by their Allies, six French tanks and two armoured personnel carriers returned, smashing through the scattered enemy troops north of the village. Major English continued: 'Whether they were the same ones that had left earlier or not it is not known.'

> They rumbled into the village and said, 'We understand that you are having a little spot of bother and we've come to help.' We thought that was the understatement of the week but they did help us considerably. When it had been decided to withdraw, we sent patrols down the side roads to see if they were clear. We put the wounded on trucks and some of the trucks had to be towed by the carriers. In fact, we got everyone

onto some sort of vehicle – some were on the French tanks – and we had six or eight men on every carrier. Nobody marched.

There were two French tanks in front and two or three more at the back. We left there at 0300 and on the journey between Warlus and Duisans we saw some German vehicles and they fired some shots but they didn't bother us very much.

Without the loyal return of the French tanks, described by the battalion's historian as 'a miracle' and the degree of surprise achieved by the break-out from the burning village, Colonel Beart's Battalion HQ and two companies would surely have been lost. What is not commonly acknowledged is that the French armour not only – as in the case of 8 DLI – facilitated their escape but generally covered the withdrawal of the British tanks and infantry.

Rommel summed up the final phase of the battle principally involving the 25th Panzer Regiment in his report: 'This action brought the enemy armour into such confusion that, in spite of their superior numbers, they fell back to Arras. Fighting ceased after nightfall. Meanwhile, the situation north-west of Wailly had been resolved [8 DLI].'

Withdrawal to Vimy Ridge

'Gun Buster' had been forward to Beaurains to recover the battery OP who had been left behind by the infantry and was now on his way back to Achicourt:

> I hadn't proceeded far before meeting signs that an entirely new situation had arisen. Towards me, down the road from Achicourt, struggled little batches of our infantry, dust-stained, grimy, some without their tin helmets and rifles, and all struggling along under a dead-weight of weariness. They displayed all the signs of a rough time. Stopping a corporal, I asked what had happened.
>
> 'The bloody tanks have smashed through us,' he said fiercely. 'We've had to withdraw. The bastards are chasing us now.'

'Gun Buster' was not inclined to believe him; however, not only were the panzers behind him but

> my heart gave a sudden bound and seemed to get stuck in my throat. Not more than three hundred yards in front, its nose pointing towards us, a stationary German tank blocked the road.
>
> 'Quick; turn her round,' I gasped. But the driver wanted no telling. He swung the car over so abruptly that the wheels almost left the ground.

He made it back to the battery gun position at Dainville but, even though he himself had been dubious about the presence of enemy tanks so far forward, he was exasperated at the incredulity of his battery commander. 'The major said he could not take the responsibility to move,' but confirmation from 'a dog-tired young subaltern who could hardly keep his eyes open as he stumbled along the road' convinced the major:

Pz IV Panzer IV.

'The Germans,' he said, 'had delivered a terrific counter-attack to the south-west of Arras with hundreds of tanks. Our infantry had been outflanked on the right and attacked in the rear. The British tanks had come up against the huge German thirty-five-ton tanks [Panzer IV] for the first time, and suffered heavy casualties. Achicourt had been outflanked, too, and the enemy was still pushing forward.'

As the battery pulled out, the first six enemy tanks could be heard and just about seen climbing up towards Dainville.

Well before dawn and the return of the *Luftwaffe*, the depleted and very weary brigade was ordered to continue its withdrawal from Marœuil to Vimy Ridge, which was carried out in some chaos but without much interference from the enemy.

151 Brigade marched to a reserve position where they held a 2-mile-long position on the forward slope of Vimy Ridge and down to the village of Givenchy, digging in with all three battalions in the line. On the left, with 151 Brigade's anti-tank company covering the Lens-Arras road, the 4 RNF held most of Bois de la Folie. In the centre, 9 DLI, with a troop of guns from 260 Anti-Tank Battery, were dug in around the Canadian Vimy Ridge Monument and a lucky company occupied the preserved First World War concrete trenches. The half of 8 DLI that had withdrawn from Duisans and further guns of 260 Anti-Tank Battery extended the line further north towards Givenchy-en-Gohelle Wood, with the 6 DLI, who had suffered worst in the previous day's operations, providing the brigade reserve to the east of the ridge in Petit Vimy.

While the infantry were taking up their positions, 'Gun Buster' was leading 386 Battery back towards their old positions near Vimy Ridge, the column of vehicles making their way through groups of weary infantry 'who begged for a lift'. Halting the column in Neuville-St Vaast he went a mile further on up onto the ridge to check out the battery's gun pits and what he saw highlights the fact that many citizens of Arras driven out of the city by the bombing on the 21st suffered cruelly:

The sight that greeted me turned my blood cold. Heaps of dead and dying men, women and children filled our gun-pits. They were refugees who had taken cover there, and been literally blasted out of life some hours earlier by German bombers, probably looking for us. From the interior of these piles of torn, limbless, decapitated bodies sounded an occasional groan where some unfortunate still drew breath. A sickening stench pervaded the warm air. Upon this spectacle of horror, the midnight moon shone brightly from a cloudless sky.

My driver and I stared at each other speechless. Our feelings were beyond words. The total absence of any sign that these poor wretches had received any assistance accentuated the horror. The mangled piles remained, after all these hours, in exactly the same state as when the bombers had finished with them. No succour, no relief, no medical attention of any sort. Even the dead had been left to choke, with the weight of their bodies, the last breath out of the injured. It was typical of the utter breakdown of the French civilian relief services all over the northern invasion area.

As dawn rose the battery was finally parked up and the exhausted gunners able to sleep but within an hour the grumbling Gunners had deployed, with an OP up by the Canadian memorial, to support 8 DLI who were being probed by German recce a couple of thousand yards to their north around Givenchy.

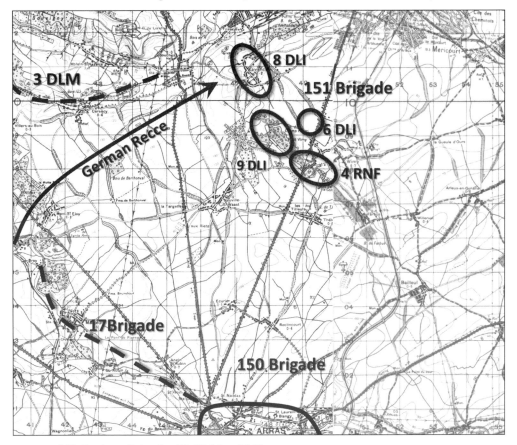

151 Durham Brigade, 22–23 May 1940.

Meanwhile, 6 DLI had the misfortune to have its column split in one of those confusions only too common in even the best-organized peacetime night march. Major Perry and nearly 200 men became separated and, believing that they were the only survivors of the battalion, headed for Boulogne where they joined the Welsh Guards in fighting for the port before being taken back to the south coast by a destroyer. The remainder of the battalion stayed with 151 Brigade. After five days of marching and battle Lieutenant Colonel Miller finally utterly exhausted himself in seeking out the brigade's main HQ and having been on a protracted hunt eventually found it – despite all rumours – in Petit Vimy, where it had always been. Such was his exhaustion and being well over 50, 'it was considered that he best return home', with Major Jeffreys left to take command. The remnants of the battalion, numbering some 200 men, were reorganized and initially of his five company commanders Major Jeffreys had four second lieutenants commanding companies, which were little more than platoon strength, and a single captain. The command situation improved as more officer stragglers rejoined over the following days.

The manning situation was better for 8 DLI when, during the course of the morning, much to the surprise of Major McLaren the rest of A and D companies, sadly depleted to 50 per cent strength, 'reappeared from the dead' to rejoin them on Vimy Ridge. Lieutenant Colonel Beart, who had been wounded in the action at Warlus, now without that adrenalin rush of battle to keep him going was reluctantly evacuated and Major McLaren took command.

Throughout the 22nd further stragglers, individuals and groups rejoined their battalions. The redoubtable Sergeant Heppel's matter-of-fact report is typical:

> I had now with me Trooper Nichol, driver of Lieut. Nugent's tank. His tank, like another Mk II I saw, had caught fire and the crew had separated. An infantry straggler made up my party to five, so securing two Bren guns, and a water bottle and rations each, we made our way into the country, halting at a ruined aerodrome about 0230 hours on the 22nd.
>
> On the following morning, I led my party into Arras. We reported to Area Headquarters and were later sent back to Vimy.

There were others such as Lieutenant Dees of 8 DLI, who had been captured in Warlus but escaped and made his way north joining other stragglers before being recaptured after fighting with GHQ troops in Hazebrouck.

Lieutenant Vaux, Major Fernie and a driver, all of 4 RTR, found themselves on foot when their tank finally broke down as a result of battle damage. After numerous encounters with the enemy overnight and losing the driver in the River Scarpe, the pair made it back to Vimy and the much-reduced regimental leaguer. Contemplating the fact that they were facing 180 degrees in the opposite direction to their First World War forebears, the Durhams received the order that 'the Ridge was to be held to the end – at all costs.'

Losses

The losses to both sides in the intense afternoon's fighting on 21 May 1940 were considerable but difficult to tie down due to the inability to keep records in a fast-developing situation.

The 7th Panzer Division's history, quoting the figures in Rommel's diary, records losses of 89 killed, 116 wounded and 173 missing, plus a considerable number of panzers and other vehicles lost and much equipment destroyed. British sources quoting 7th Panzer Division's war diary stated the loss of nine medium and several light tanks, 378 men killed or wounded and 173 missing; British records state that almost 400 Germans were taken prisoner. To reconcile German statements with the numbers missing and the British claim of prisoners taken, one must conclude that a high proportion of the prisoners were released or escaped during the withdrawal back to Vimy Ridge. The history of 6 DLI records that one platoon of C Company 'had gone off earlier escorting about one hundred German prisoners'. Most 'were themselves taken prisoner by a German armoured reconnaissance unit, which in the dark had been mistaken for French'.

Altogether 7th Panzer Division suffered the heaviest casualties of any panzer division during the course of the 1940 campaign, with 2,160 casualties including 682 killed in action. This was the cost of Rommel's driving personality, risk-taking and the 'Arras counter-attack', but success in battle normally comes at a price and as Napoleon said, 'You have to break eggs to make omelettes'.

With regard to British losses, Frankforce had sixty tanks abandoned or knocked out of the eighty-eight tanks involved in the operation. 4 RTR alone lost twenty-five tanks of the three types to the guns of the 78th Artillery Regiment on Telegraph Hill, most of which were from A and D squadrons; 1 Army Tank Brigade was left with only twenty-eight tanks. Infantry losses were around 100 men killed or wounded in the attack, and it is unknown how many French soldiers became casualties in the operation.

The Matilda II tank: proof against all but the 88mm, this tank suffered a mobility kill when its track was hit.

Chapter 10

Aftermath of Battle

In the aftermath of the 'Arras counter-attack' events moved swiftly both on the ground and up the chain of command, particularly in Berlin, with the action of 21 May 1940 playing no small part in shaping subsequent events.

The German spearheads had reached the sea near Abbeville on the evening of 20 May and the BEF along with the French northern armies were ordered to withdraw to the Escaut Canal and conform with the Belgians to their north. Once in position they were to hold the line there. The overall situation at the time, as the French ability to understand what was going on and to exercise command spread to Whitehall and the BEF, is summed up by the official historian Major Ellis:

> The normal order of things was in fact reversed, and while Cabinet, Councils, Conferences and High Commanders decided what must be done to meet the overall situation as they saw it, subordinate commanders in the field decided what could be done, and countered each order of the High Command why it could not be carried out. And always in the end it was always the subordinate commanders' views that prevailed.

Ellis went on to say: 'Vigorous splashing at the centre produced only feeble ripples at the circumference.' In practice orders were watered down and exhortations to 'fight like tigers were, alas, to prove no substitute for definite and practical orders.'

Of the German panzer divisions that had dashed from the Meuse, with the vast bulk of the non-motorized infantry still lagging far behind, two were on the coast preparing to strike towards the Channel ports and two divisions had been redirected east to form defensive flanks facing north and east as a result of the 'counter-attack'. The 5th and 7th Panzer divisions along with the *SS Totenkopf* (motorized infantry) had almost enveloped Arras from the east on the River Scarpe through south to the west of the city where they still held the bridgehead over the Scarpe that the 25th Panzer Regiment had seized during the afternoon of the 21st. The Germans were firmly behind the BEF and across the British lines of communication and other than the allied troops around Arras,

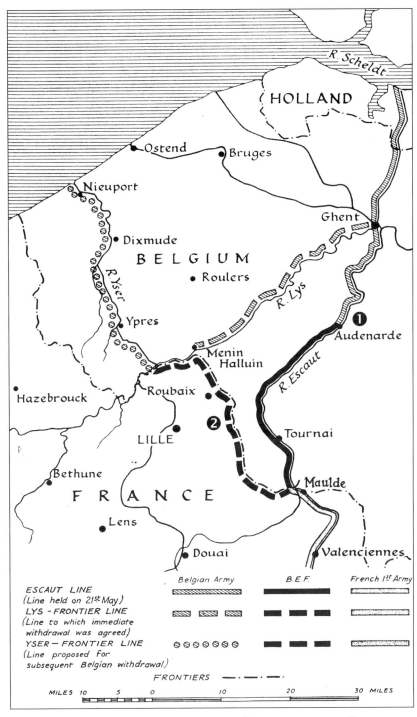

R. Scheldt

HOLLAND

Ostend

Bruges

Nieuport

Ghent

Dixmude

BELGIUM

Roulers

R. Yser

R. Lys

Ypres

❶

Audenarde

Menin
Halluin

R. Escaut

Hazebrouck

Roubaix

❷

Tournai

LILLE

Bethune

Maulde

F R A N C E

Lens

Douai

Valenciennes

	Belgian Army	B.E.F.	French 1ˢᵗ Army
ESCAUT LINE (Line held on 21ˢᵗ May)			
LYS - FRONTIER LINE (Line to which immediate withdrawal was agreed)			
YSER — FRONTIER LINE (Line proposed for subsequent Belgian withdrawal)			

FRONTIERS —·—·—·—

MILES 10   5   0   10   20   30 MILES

Withdrawal of the BEF to the Escaut Canal ❶ and the Frontier ❷.

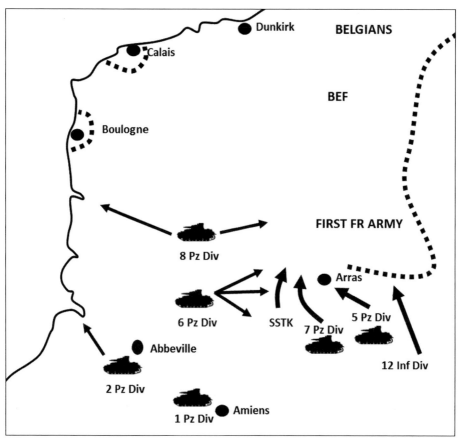

German deployment west of the BEF.

which were in danger of being surrounded, there were few troops in position to oppose the Germans between Arras and the sea during 22 May, although Prioux was in the process of regrouping his cavalry corps.

At the higher level during 22 May Churchill and Field Marshal Sir John Dill flew to Paris to meet General Weygand and the French Supreme War Council. The plan they came up with was, in summary, an attack by eight British and French divisions, on 23 June, from the north towards Cambrai and Bapaume. Lord Gort was also told 'that the new French Army Group which is advancing upon Amiens and forming a line along the Somme should strike northwards and join hands with the British divisions who are attacking southwards.'

General Weygand.

However, the Weygand Plan, like its predecessors, was impossible to execute. Even the normally reserved official historian could not resist commenting '…at no time in history could eight divisions – 100,000 men

– facing east and already engaged with the enemy march away and attack south-west with so little preparation.' The plan as conveyed was hopelessly unrealistic, redolent of moving counters on a simple board game or Hitler during his final days in the bunker.

On the 22nd, to the east, the BEF was struggling to prevent a breakthrough by Army Group B, as it fell back to the frontier line, let alone disengage and change its front. Around Arras following the previous day's battle German operations were more circumspect. With the advantage of fighting from an urban area, Petreforce was still holding out but the line of the Scarpe astride the city was under pressure, particularly to the west. 151 Brigade was technically in reserve on Vimy Ridge with the enemy some distance in front of them, initially focusing on establishing bridgeheads across the River Scarpe held by 17 Brigade of the 5th Division and heading north. However, over the next thirty-six hours 151 Brigade increasingly found itself in action as the Germans sought to outflank Arras.

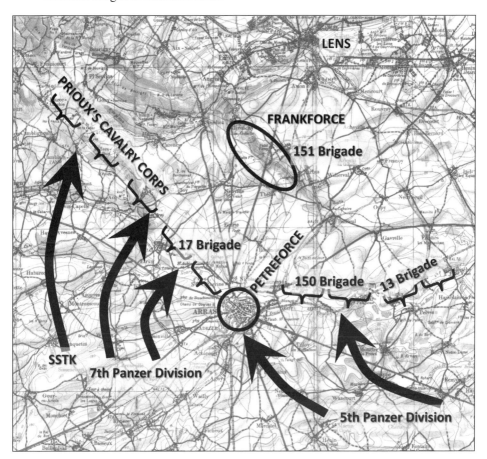

The situation around Arras, 22 May 1940.

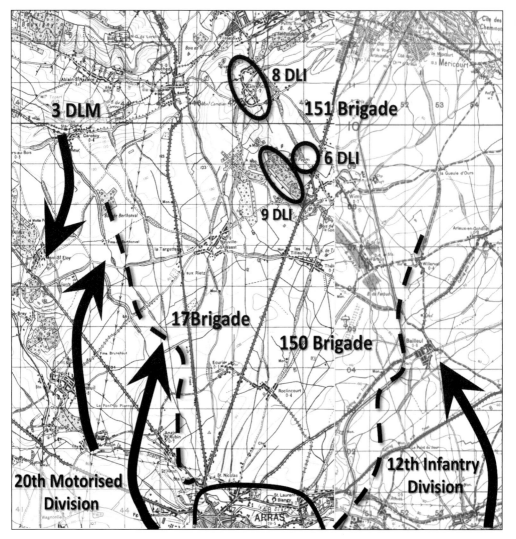

151 Durham Brigade, 22–23 May 1940.

While some infantry were lucky enough to return to the trenches they had prepared two days earlier, others dug in anew, and 'Gun Buster' established himself in the tower of the Warden's House near the Canadian Vimy Ridge Memorial. Overlooking the Scarpe and open country to the west he recalled having a relatively quiet day 'except for the huge flights of German bombers continually passing overhead on their way to bomb Lens'.

> Our guns at Givenchy were now roaring, shelling Mont St-Eloi, and Marœuil, which only a few hours previously had been our own regimental headquarters. Towards evening a special target cropped up. I spotted a German battery of four guns in front of a wood on the skyline.

Four little equidistant flashes gave them away. I telephoned the data to the Battery Command Post, the targets were plotted on the map, and as they were out of range from our present gun positions [probably south of the St. Pol Road], Ritchie, L-Troop's GPO [Gun Position Officer], was sent up with a section of two guns to a forward position three miles away to conduct the strafe. His orders were to go into action at once, fire twenty rounds per gun at the target, and hop back again.

3rd DLM were still deployed holding a line north of the Scarpe in the face of the 7th Panzer Division and the *SSTK*. It was in this battle, ignoring boundaries, that the inexperienced 386 Battery had intervened. French observers on the high ground above the village of Carency, seeing the section of L Troop moving forward, mistook it for the enemy and engaged with a battery of First World War-vintage 75mm guns. The British section was lucky to get away and back to the Givenchy area without casualties.

General Prioux, having concentrated his previously scattered corps to the west of Arras, launched a limited attack on Mont-St. Eloi with elements of the 1st and 2nd DLM with 3rd DLM covering the flanks. The 1st/4th Regiment Dragoons Portée, infantry mounted in Citroën Chenilettes (light armoured half-tracks), led the attack and were supported by some H-35 tanks of the 18th Dragoons. It was successful in securing the village and the dominating ruins of the abbey overlooking the Scarpe and drove the Germans back across the river between Écoivres and Bray.

The 7th Panzer Division's casualty bill, mainly fighting the French during 22 May, was 5 officers, 5 senior NCOs and 90 men killed, wounded and missing. Although only half that of the previous day, it was one of the higher daily totals of the entire campaign.

Withdrawal to the Canal Line

During 23 June, the pressure around Arras mounted steadily and both the British and French were pushed back. With the arrival of the first of their infantry divisions, the panzers could be redirected into country more suitable for them. 11 *Schützen* Brigade was to continue the attack on Arras and leading elements of the 20th Motorised Division were to maintain pressure on 17 Brigade (5th Division), now deployed forward of 151 Brigade, between the city and Mont-St. Eloi. This would enable the 5th and 7th Panzer divisions and the *SSTK* to resume their advance north towards Béthune. During the course of the day the advance of the panzers left the British around Arras outflanked to the west and in danger of envelopment.

Meanwhile, in depth behind 17 Brigade, up in the tower of the warden's residence 'Gun Buster' had a good view of the fighting on the open country below. With the withdrawal of 17 Brigade and the 3rd DLM being pushed back the battle line, which the afternoon before had been roughly about 6,000 yards from the Ridge, had by now approached to within 2,000 yards, except in the centre where the salient towards Arras still jutted out. From each flank, the roar and rattle of the fighting grew in intensity. You could see the tracer shells of the anti-tank guns firing at the German tanks quite plainly, and the spurts of machine-gun fire, and tiny figures of men running hither and thither every now and then, in and out of the curtain of smoke.

We did a couple of useful shoots that morning. An enemy tank concentration was reported in a wood near Mont-St. Eloi. We worked the target out off the map and fired a salvo which apparently caught the tanks just as they were emerging from the wood. Four out of the twelve were knocked out, and the others retreated. Later on, we shelled big enemy infantry concentrations in Mont-St. Eloi itself, watching through our glasses with great satisfaction our own shells bursting in their midst.

Clearly the Germans were not having things entirely their own way but they were making steady progress towards Vimy Ridge and it certainly doesn't seem to have entered 'Gun Buster's' mind that 151 Brigade had been ordered to hold Vimy Ridge 'to the last man and last round'.

During the 22nd and into the 23rd the main problem for the Durham infantry was attack by the *Luftwaffe*, which could not always easily discriminate between troops and refugees moving around the area. 6 DLI, who were the brigade reserve, record burying civilian casualties, mainly people heading north from Arras. 8 DLI in Givenchy saw 'several carts loaded with refugees receive direct hits as they passed through the village. When the smoke and dust had cleared away the long column of refugees moved on again beyond the bomb craters and wreckage out into the country.'

A knocked out early war version of a Panzer IV with its low velocity 75mm gun.

Despite his 'the last man and last round', with the danger of losing both the 5th and 50th divisions around Arras, Lord Gort abandoned any intention of executing the Weygand Plan to attack south. During the day to the east of the city the enemy had crossed the Scarpe, penetrated between 13 and 150 brigades forcing them back and with 17 Brigade similarly forced back, the end of the defence of Arras was in sight. Consequently, on the evening of 23 May he made the decision to withdraw the 5th Division and Petreforce from the all but surrounded Arras using the roads through Petit Vimy and Givenchy. Inevitably they attracted the attention of the *Luftwaffe*. 8 DLI historian records the passage of an RASC convoy and that

Lt. Furness VC.

several of the trucks were set on fire and whilst the troops fought the flames a direct hit set the village school blazing and some sheds nearby where the Battalion cooks' truck had been hidden…several large bombs fell in the courtyard of the village church killing some of the battalion's signallers.

Among those wounded were two battery commanders of the 50th Division's anti-tank regiment, the Norfolk Yeomanry.

As an example of the situation around Arras, particularly to the east of the city during the withdrawal of Petreforce from Arras, Lieutenant the Hon. Christopher Furness, the carrier platoon commander of 1 Welsh Guards, was awarded a posthumous Victoria Cross for his action with the rear guard. At around 0230 hours he commanded three surviving carriers on the road from Arras to Vimy. His citation reads as follows:

Victoria Cross.

His extremely high degree of leadership and dash imbued his command with a magnificent offensive spirit during their constant patrols and many local actions throughout this period. On May 22nd, 1940, he was wounded, but refused to be evacuated. The enemy had encircled the town on three sides, and Lt. Furness's platoon, together with a small force of light tanks, were ordered to cover the withdrawal of over 40 transport vehicles to Douai. Heavy small arms and anti-tank gun fire blocked the column. Lt. Furness, realising the seriousness of the situation, with three carriers and the light tanks attacked at close quarters

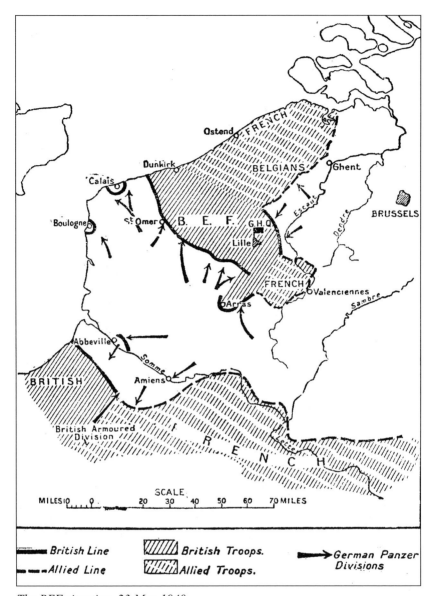

The BEF situation, 23 May 1940.

the strongly entrenched enemy, inflicting heavy losses. His carriers were hit, most of their crews killed or wounded, and the tanks were put out of action. When his own carrier was disabled and the driver and gunner killed, Lt. Furness, despite his wounds, engaged the enemy in hand to hand combat until he was killed. His magnificent act of self-sacrifice against hopeless odds made the enemy withdraw long enough to allow the large transport column to get clear unmolested, and to permit the evacuation of some of the wounded of his own platoon and of the light tanks.

Once 5th Division was clear of Arras and north of Vimy, orders came that the Durham Brigade, who were relieved that they were not to fight 'to the last round', was to withdraw to the north overnight on 23/24 May. They were to head to the Ypres area where another crisis was facing the BEF. Meanwhile, 18 miles to the north of Arras, a new defence was to be mounted on the Canal d'Aire and the La Bassée Canal by Polforce, a force that was originally intended to deploy around St. Pol but had been overtaken by the speed of the panzers' advance on 20 May.

Once 17 Brigade had been steadily pushed back from Marœuil towards the northern outskirts of Arras and joined the withdrawal, the Durhams, now effectively in the front line, deployed a screen of outposts forward, principally provided by their carrier platoons. As night fell, however, the tempo of German operations slackened, probably because the 20th Motorised Division was ordered in the next twenty-four hours to head north to join the panzers on the coast.

Colonel Percy, CO of 9 DLI who were up on Vimy Ridge, recalled:

> About 1 a.m. [24 May], after an urgent summons to Brigade HQ, I was told the line was to retire and that I had to withdraw my Battalion forthwith to 20 miles behind the La Bassée Canal. Here was a nice situation. Owing to having been told several times that there would be no withdrawal, I had no transport for all the stuff I had dumped and, under the conditions, it was impossible to get the vehicles back in time. There was no time to organise the withdrawal properly in the dark but we managed to get some of our equipment and stores put on vehicles of attached units but the men had to carry all the Bren guns, anti-tank rifles and small mortars, plus ammunition, back a distance of nearly 20 miles.

Captain Harry Sell, the brigade's Mechanised Transport Officer, in taking a final walk around the abandoned defences discovered that men had been left behind with 'two happy souls still blissfully sleeping' in a trench. In going through the blazing buildings of Givenchy to check for stragglers, in the firelight he spotted a German reconnaissance patrol coming the other way through what had been 8 DLI's depth positions, so 'he beat a hasty retreat.' Catching up with the column heading north he halted on the road outside the village where he found '8th Battalion's mess vehicles with the exhausted cooks snoring peacefully within'. Shouts of 'Boche tanks!' galvanized them into action.

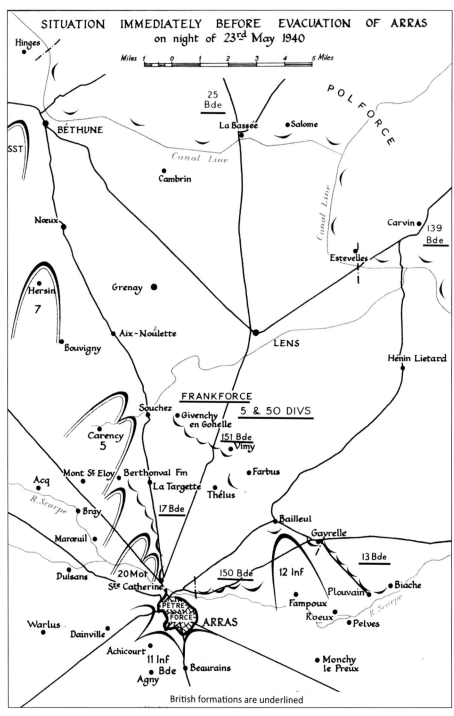

The situation on the evening of 23 May 1940.

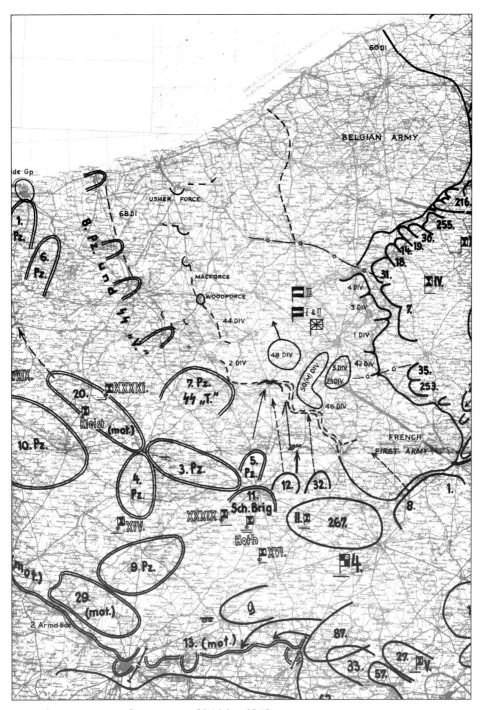

The situation on the evening of 24 May 1940.

9 DLI were luckier:

We got clear of the Ridge just before dawn but, although the enemy did not follow up, it was a desperate march for the wretched men carrying such heavy loads. However, they stuck to it amazingly well and all got back over the Canal before the bridges were blown. We had to leave a lot of stores and equipment on the Ridge – also, incidentally, a party of about six cooks were also left, as they had gone off somewhere to sleep in a shell hole in the trees and could not be found before the withdrawal – they must have had a surprise awakening in the morning – we have since heard they are prisoners of war.

Chapter 11

The Canal Line

As the panzers raced across the BEF's lines of communication to the sea, carving through scattered rear-echelon formations and units, during 20 May Lord Gort ordered Major General Curtis to form a line along the series of canals that stretched in a generally south-easterly direction from Gravelines on the coast down towards Béthune and then east towards Lille. This 50-mile line was at first held by a handful of battalions of Polforce from 25 Brigade of 46th Division, a second line Territorial Force division, which was one of the three low establishment lines of communication formations in the BEF. Polforce was supplemented by a variety of ad hoc companies, including some made up of personnel in transit to and from leave plus a searchlight unit. With so few troops, all General Curtis could do was to concentrate on holding the bridges. One weak battalion of 25 Brigade, for instance, held crossings on no less than 6 miles of the Canal Line!

8th Panzer Division had reached the canal in the Arques–St. Omer area during the night of 22/23 May, arriving at a key bridge just before a chemical company of Royal Engineers. The sappers eventually managed to drive a truck rigged with explosives onto the bridge but the resulting detonation only damaged it; sufficiently, however, to prevent panzers from crossing. Elsewhere along this sector of the Canal Line the ad hoc defence companies, supported by single 25-pounders of 392 Battery Royal Artillery, held attacks by elements of the 8th Panzer's infantry and pioneers at seven bridges for most of the day. This largely forgotten action by 'unglamorous troops', along with that of the 68th French Infantry Division further north, undoubtedly prevented von Rundstedt ordering a German drive on Dunkirk that would have cut the BEF off from the coast. Instead on 23 June he instructed General Hoth to 'first clear up the situation at Arras and only then push on to Calais and Boulogne.'

In the east with the BEF falling back to the Franco-Belgian frontier during 23–24 May the 2nd, 44th and 48th divisions were relieved by the French who supposed that they would be used by the British in their part of the Weygand Plan. Lord Gort, however, deployed them to the Canal Line where the ad hoc units of Polforce were continuing to resist German pressure. Major General Irwin's 2nd Infantry Division was still moving into position when 151 Durham Brigade crossed the Aire/La Bassée Canal late on the 24th.

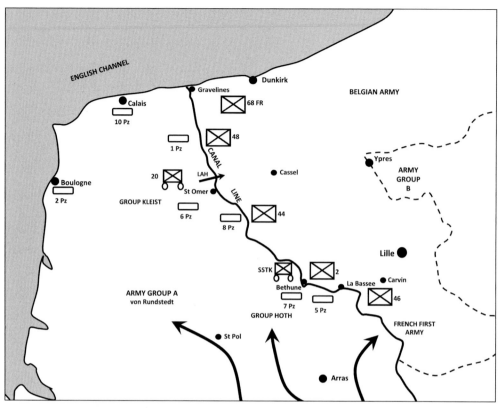

The Canal Line and Allied deployment to the east of the water feature.

Meanwhile, with the reduction in the tempo of German operations as they reached the sea and reacted to the 'Arras counter-attack', the infantry divisions started to close up with von Kluge urging them on. They were, however, still widely spread and fear had grown in the upper levels of the German command of a full-blown Allied counter offensive against their spearheads in northern France. On the afternoon of 24 May Berlin issued the infamous *Haltbefehl* or 'Halt Order' (see Appendix IV). General Heinz Guderian, who normally had plenty to say, was reported as being speechless; to commanders at the front the order was incomprehensible. Guderian later wrote:

> On this day [the 24th] the Supreme Command intervened in the operations in progress, with results which were to have a most disastrous influence on the whole future course of the war. Hitler ordered the left wing to stop on the Aa. It was forbidden to cross that stream. We were not informed of the reasons for this. The order contained the words: 'Dunkirk is to be left to the *Luftwaffe*. Should the capture of Calais prove difficult, this port too is to be left to the *Luftwaffe*' (I quote here from memory). We were utterly speechless. But since we were not informed of the reasons for this order, it was difficult to argue against it. The panzer divisions were therefore instructed: 'Hold the line of the canal. Make use of the period of rest for general recuperation.'

In some places, the canal had already been crossed and therefore bridgeheads were given up and German troops withdrew back cross the canal. Hitler's bodyguard, the *Leibstandarte* (LAH) under *Obergruppenführer* Sepp Dietrich, organised as a motorized infantry regiment, at this stage, however, ignored the order and conducted an attack on Mont Watten, a significant feature just north of St. Omer.

As far as the British on the Canal Line were concerned the Halt Order enabled 151 Brigade to get back and for other troops to move into position under the command, as initially intended, of III Corps. In the end it was Major General Eastwood, a member of the GHQ Staff, with another extemporised headquarters who took charge of the defences.

The 2nd Division, with 2 Light Reconnaissance Brigade under command, now organized as a composite regiment, was to hold the 15-mile sector from Aire-sur-la-Lys to La Bassée but during the 24th, particularly around Aire, they had to fight through German outposts to reach it. To their east they were to replace French Algerian troops that held the area around La Bassée and a battalion of the Queen's Regiment (Polforce). The 46th Division was to be concentrated under General Curtis around Carvin, while to the north of Aire-sur-la-Lys the 44th Division came into the line. The 48th Division held positions

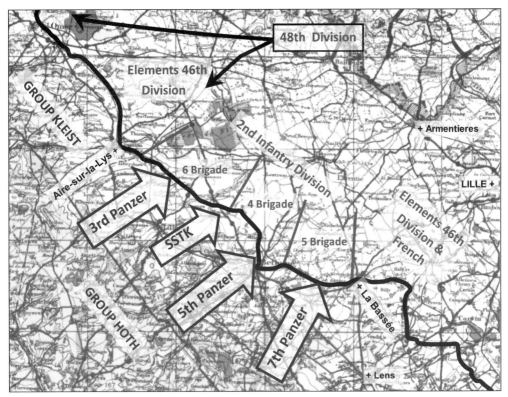

The 2nd Division on the Canal Line.

Infantry of the 2nd Division on the march.

north to the sea including key terrain such as Mont Cassel. Facing the 2nd Division by last light on 24 May were, around Béthune, leading elements of the *SSTK* and shortly afterwards Rommel's 7th Panzer Division, while to the east the foremost units of the 5th Panzer Division were coming into contact around Béthune.

See map on page 156.

2 Dorsets' war diary for 24 May records that 'On passing through La Bassée women and children refugees were laying on the pavements, where they had been machine-gunned by the Germans.'

The 2nd Division, which had two Territorial battalions in its ranks alongside the regulars, deployed all three of its brigades into the line, with 5 Brigade holding the sector from east of Béthune via Point Fixe to the western outskirts of La Bassée. 7 Worcesters, one of the division's Territorial battalions, held position on the left, forward on 2 miles of canal bank, and 2 Dorsets were resting in the village of Festubert 1 mile north of the canal. 1 Queen's Own Cameron Highlanders were 5 Brigade's reserve battalion. In the 5 Brigade area, there was an extensive area of marsh, ponds and drainage ditches which at first was regarded as being an unlikely avenue of approach for the Germans, hence only one battalion being initially deployed forward. Of great significance to coming events was that the area of the bend in the canal facing Béthune was held by 1/8 Lancashire Fusiliers, the division's second Territorial battalion, belonging to 4 Brigade. There were also detachments of a French motorized battalion sited along the canal.

The 2nd Division, despite the *Haltbefehl*, was not to have a quiet time. As far as the German commanders were concerned, the order was to allow the infantry divisions to catch up and it certainly didn't preclude such operations that would improve their position when the leashes were released. During 25 and 26 May, 5 Brigade would consequently see plenty of action, as they were – unknown to them – positioned on Group Hoth's *schwerpunkt*, where Hoth was intending to attack as soon as the *Haltbefehl* was lifted. The three thinly-spread brigades of the 2nd Division would ultimately face the overwhelming might of three panzer divisions and the *Totenkopf* Division. In other words, although there would be few surprises in what was now a more conventional operation. The Germans had assembled a critical mass on this sector of the La Bassée Canal.

With the decision eventually being made to withdraw to Dunkirk and evacuation, for the 2nd Division and those others fighting to hold the western Allied flank there was no question of withdrawal; they would be the rear guard to hold and delay the Germans as long as possible.

Over the night of 24/25 May the 4th Panzer Division (replacing 5th Panzer) arrived on the banks of the canal and immediately set about reconnaissance. One patrol at dawn was reported as 'an attack' by some French troops and stragglers from the Royal Irish Fusiliers, saying that the enemy was in possession of half the hamlet of Gorre. D Company, 2 Dorsets was tasked to

The 7th Worcesters on mobilization in 1939.

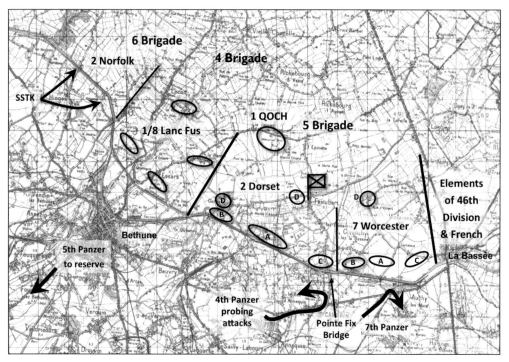

5 Brigade on the Canal Line, 24–25 May 1940.

counter-attack; however, finding nothing but observing plenty of activity on the far bank, they returned to report. Shortly afterwards at 0800 hours, the 2nd Dorsets were ordered forward to dig in on the canal bank, with three companies forward on a 3-mile frontage. Due to a lack of firm ground and fields of fire, positions were mainly on the towpath and in adjacent buildings.

During the day, there was a vigorous exchange of artillery and mortar fire across the canal. 2 Dorsets' historian wrote:

> The Germans from their excellent observation posts on the slag heaps were able to direct intense and most accurate mortar and gun fire… The Battalion were by now becoming accustomed, if not inured, to the precision of the German mortarmen, and in order to try to combat this menace tried out an old trick learnt when fighting against the Arabs in Palestine. They mounted a 3-inch mortar on a 15-cwt. truck and used this in a counter-mortar role with most satisfactory effect.

During the day A Company in the centre had become effectively isolated from Battalion Headquarters and pinned down by enemy fire from close quarters, where concealed riflemen came into their own and the Dorsets digging in just 25 yards away across the canal made easy targets:

> The banks of the canal provided some cover and platoons were busy during the morning digging into the bank themselves. However, on the

south bank of the canal, opposite the 'B' Company front, was a French train which had long been stationary. Into this train the Germans were finding their way, and by taking advantage of the few feet of extra height thus gained were rapidly developing sniper superiority on this part of the front. A call was sent to the Battalion mortars, who brought down a most successful concentration on this train and set it alight. It turned out to be an ammunition train full of all types of ammunition which continued to blaze for the next two days.

With the battalion dug in, during the afternoon panzers were seen massing near the bridge at Pointe Fixe held by C Company, which had been kept open until the last moment to allow rear guards and stragglers to get across the canal to rejoin the BEF. Under the cover of smoke *Schützen-Regiment* 12 and 1 *Kompanie*, Pioneer Battalion 79 attempted to seize the bridge before it was blown but failed. The 2nd Division's engineers and the infantry's assault pioneers had done a good job in blowing all the bridges on the division's front.

The Germans used the period of the *Haltbefehl* to indulge in psychological operations. The reaction was somehow predictable: 'To add interest to the day's proceedings, the enemy started dropping invitations to desert… Needless to say, this addition of otherwise useless paper was much appreciated by a battalion whose domestic stores were well-nigh exhausted.'

La Bassée Canal near Cuinchy in the 2nd Dorsets' sector.

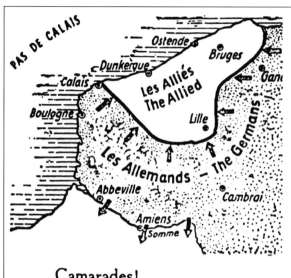

One of the leaflets dropped on the 2nd Dorsets. Compare this with the map on page 150.

Camarades!

Telle est la situation!
En tout cas, la guerre est finie pour vous!
Vos chefs vont s'enfuir par avion.
A bas les armes!

British Soldiers!

Look at this map: it gives your true situation!
Your troops are entirely surrounded —
stop fighting!
Put down your arms!

A lack of essential paper was not the only logistical problem facing 5 Brigade. With frequent moves over the previous days, refugees clogging up the roads and the *Luftwaffe* bombing and strafing convoys, the supply system had broken down and the brigade was on half-rations. Consequently, the battalions record that they were 'living off the land', taking anything they could find from abandoned houses and farms.

During the course of 26 May, the shelling and mortaring continued but further to the east 7 Worcesters were in action against the 7th Panzer Division. The Worcesters' war diary gives a feel for the day:

Battalion held line of canal. Enemy activity increased – heavy shelling and mortar fire intermittently all day. Many casualties…

    Battalion badly situated, having practically no field of fire, and no observation. All our posts could be observed from enemy vantage points on southern side of canal, and by enemy reconnaissance plane flying over our positions during all hours of daylight. During the late afternoon or evening some enemy must have crossed the canal in the centre of our front. On recce, and while trying to locate 'A' Company's position, Commanding Officer, 2IC, IO, and 2/Lieut. Goodwin came upon an enemy post, which opened fire and wounded the 2IC, (Major Goldie), and IO (2/Lieut. Woodward). During the night one company 1st Camerons made a counter-attack on our left, but failed to make contact with the enemy, who were reported to have crossed the canal.

It was, however, across the brigade's westerly boundary that the most significant events of the day took place. The 4th Panzer Division's probing actions, having been rebuffed by the Dorsets the day before and no doubt finding the marshy ground to the south of the canal unsuitable, they turned their attentions further to the west. They would mount their crossing in the bend of the canal from the cover of Béthune late on 26 May.

    The 2nd Dorsets' adjutant noted in the battalion's war diary on the evening of the 26th: '2115hrs approximately 60 casualties since 0900 hrs 25th May.'

A Wehrmacht *medic treats a casualty under fire.*

An SS Totenkopf *section in France during the 1940 campaign. The Waffen SS were leaders in the introduction of camouflage clothing. In this case an oversmock and helmet cover.*

Lifting the *Haltbefehl*

After much argument and a forty-eight-hour pause in operations, during which many of the infantry formations had marched hard to close up, Hitler lifted the *Haltbefehl* on the afternoon of 26 May, but by the time the order had been passed down the chain of command to divisions in most cases it was too late to mount serious attacks on the Canal Line. Not so, however, for Group Hoth. Both the 4th and 7th Panzer divisions had been securing positions, manoeuvring and grouping for a resumption of the offensive, and the *SSTK* were already across the canal and fighting 6 Brigade to the north of Béthune.

Now concentrated and facing 7 Worcesters, Rommel recorded that:

> According to air reports which came in to my headquarters on the afternoon of the 26th May, the enemy had been observed north of the canal withdrawing towards the north-west. I immediately requested permission from Corps to drive a bridgehead over the canal that evening. It was soon granted.
>
> I remained with the troops on the canal all the evening. The *Aufklärungsabteilung* 37 [Reconnaissance Battalion], although suffering severely from the activities of snipers, succeeded, with artillery help, in pushing armoured patrols through as far as the canal, but strong enemy resistance prevented the creation of a bridgehead. *Schützenregiment* 7, however, achieved a notable success that evening by getting elements of both its battalions across the La Bassée canal, which was blocked by immense numbers of sunken barges. After eliminating a number of

enemy machine-gun nests, both battalions established themselves on the northern bank. Apart from a few casualties at the crossing point caused by flanking fire from British machine-gun posts to the west, the creation of the bridgehead at this point seemed to have caused no great difficulty and there was now good reason to expect that the battalions would establish a strong position on the northern bank during the night.

Troops of 7th Panzer Division are reported at one stage to have attempted to approach the bridge in La Bassée, which was just across the boundary in 46th Division's area, using civilians as cover. This may have been an attempt by Rommel's recce to 'bounce' the defenders. 7 Worcesters' history, probably referring to *Schützenregiment* 7's bridgehead, records that 'a message from Captain Tomkinson came in saying that "C" Company was completely surrounded, but that he was hanging on as long as possible, and in this situation a sorely wounded battalion fought on through to the following morning.'

A Company could also not be contacted. The situation was looking grim for the Worcesters.

Meanwhile, across the brigade boundary 4th Panzer Division had mounted an attack across the western loop of the canal from Béthune. *Schützenregiment* 12, the engineer battalion and the Panzer Pioneer battalion, supported by machine guns, anti-tank guns and artillery, assaulted at 2045 hours, initially without the normal preliminary bombardment. This took the 1/8th Lancashire

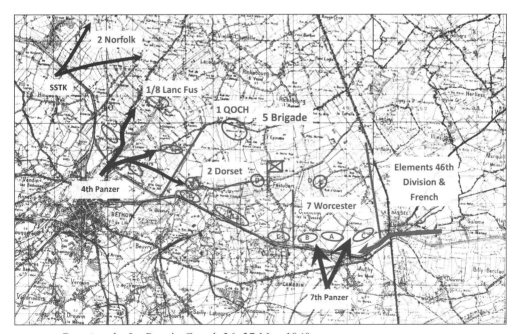

Crossing the La Bassée Canal, 26–27 May 1940.

German Pioneers in action on the Canal Line ferrying a 75mm infantry gun.

Fusiliers by surprise and they promptly lost forty men as prisoners to the Germans. By 2300 hours, advancing with the aid of copious artillery fire, they had reached the 'short cut' arm of the canal, a distance of 1,000 yards. Overnight their *Pioneeren* built a pair of bridges: an 8-ton and a 16-ton. They would, however, still have to cross the 'short cut' canal the following morning.

The Worcesters' war diary records that the 27th started well with 5 Brigade's reserve battalion, along with six French tanks, in support in action in their area. 'In the early morning one Company of 1 Camerons, with French tanks, swept along the canal bank and reported a few enemy who retired across the canal.' However, as the morning wore on there was far less good news:

> The Carrier Platoon was sent for from Rear HQ and were heavily bombed and shelled, suffering some casualties, losing two Carriers. Contact was made with enemy tanks and information as to enemy movements secured. No information received from 'A' Company since the previous night, presumably they were over-run. Of 'C' Company on the left there was no trace, and they must have suffered the same fate.

Rommel wrote that among the preparations made by the 7th Panzer Division the previous day and overnight:

The Engineer Battalion had constructed a number of pontoons in a small harbour just off the canal, sufficient to build a bridge. However, they had built the 8-ton type instead of the long 16-tons, as the latter would have been too difficult to manoeuvre through the litter of submerged or semi-submerged barges which was blocking the canal. The sappers had already tried to blast a way through with explosives, but with little success, due to the unwieldiness of the sunken barges.

Despite the earlier sweep along the canal, it seemed to 5 Brigade that on their left there was probably very little standing in the way of 7th Panzer Division and so it proved. Rommel, nonetheless, reported:

Prospects did not look too good for the attack across the canal. Elements of the 2nd Battalion *Schützenregiment* 7 had crossed in rubber boats and were now located on the opposite bank in bushes close to the canal. The battalion had not, however, as I had wished, extended its hold deeper on the north bank and dug itself in, nor had it taken the village of Givenchy. It had also omitted to clean up the enemy for a few hundred yards along the north bank to the west, and to get anti-tank guns and heavy weapons across and dig them in. The fire protection of the heavy company on the south bank was also inadequate.

A Panzer II of 7th Panzer Division crossing the canal at La Bassée.

Schützenregiment 7's 1st Battalion similarly held a small bridgehead further east towards La Bassée. 7 Worcesters committed their reserve and for a time held the Germans. Their view of this situation was that

> The enemy in strong force, with tanks, succeeded in crossing canal in the centre left of GIVENCHY. 'D' Company, who were on the right, were flanked by the enemy and made GIVENCHY a strongpoint, holding this village with about 70 men until 1530 hrs that day. Considerable casualties were inflicted on enemy infantry, but not without severe casualties to this Company.

Meanwhile, to 5 Brigade's right flank 4 Brigade was attacked at 0430 hours by infantry; dive-bombers and artillery covered an assault across the 'short cut' arm of the canal by infantry. Line communications between the battalions and 4 Brigade's HQ were cut by artillery and mortar fire and they resorted to radios, which with overcrowded frequencies and possibly jamming as well proved to be tenuous. The companies were well dug in but the Germans began to slip round them, forcing Brigadier Warren, with little defensive power of his own, to move his headquarters back to Lestrem and beyond the Béthune-Estaires Canal. As with 7 Worcesters, the forward battalion held out but at 1200 hours contact was lost with the 1 Lancashire Fusiliers and shortly afterwards their depth battalion, 1 Royal Scots, as well. Runners were sent with orders for the two battalions to withdraw behind the Lys Canal but either they never got through or the battalions were unable to move. At around 1530 hours contact was lost with 2 Norfolks; most of the brigade had been overwhelmed by 4th Panzer Division. Only a handful of machine-gun and mortar detachments of 2 Manchesters and stragglers from the three battalions remained with Brigade HQ.

In the centre of 5 Brigade's area, 2 Dorsets had already sent back their administrative echelon the previous evening and Battalion Headquarters was operating from a substantial First World War pillbox. Lieutenant Colonel Stephenson was immediately aware that his battalion was in danger of being outflanked or even enveloped as the Germans penetrated through the 1 Lancashire Fusiliers on an axis via Le Hamel and Lonçon, reaching to within approximately 1,000 yards of Battalion HQ in Festubert.

Between 0530 and 0730 hours, Colonel Stephenson sent the two platoons of D Company along with the carrier platoon and two attached Vickers gun sections to the east to support B Company on the western edge of Gorre Wood where the enemy's advance presented an immediate threat to the battalion. The Germans reacted swiftly with machine guns and mortars, causing casualties to the Dorsets moving in the open but the battalion's flank had been stabilized. Behind them, elements of the brigade reserve (1 QOCH) attempted to block 4th Panzer's advance to the north-east but nonetheless the Germans made steady progress on their main axis behind the Dorsets.

SS Assault Pioneers launching a rubber boat north of Béthune.

German infantrymen advancing beyond the canal at Béthune.

From 0730 hours, 5 Brigade was under air attack in preparation for 4th Panzer's next battle to break out from the bridgehead across the 'short cut' canal, which was being bridged with a 20-ton span allowing panzers up to the weight of a battle-laden Panzer III to cross and come into action against 5 Brigade. The attack began at 0800 hours, with B Company 2 Dorsets reporting that enemy infantry in company-strength *Schützenregiment* 12 had formed up approximately 300 yards from Gorre village in a ditch. It is recorded in the regimental history that

> Sergeant Cooper, of the Carrier Platoon, had managed to get up to B Company area with two carriers loaded with ammunition. Captain John Heron, the company second-in-command, volunteered to man Cooper's carriers and counter-attack to break up this outflanking movement. Sam Symes [officer commanding D Company] agreed to this, and this attack was a complete success...
>
> Later in the morning, when the Boche had re-formed in this same area and were attempting to repeat their earlier manoeuvre, Sergeant Cooper once more sallied out and dispersed the attack, returning with bits of dead German in his carrier tracks. Sergeant Cooper's gallantry and initiative during the hectic hours of that morning at Gorre, and his constant and successful management of the carriers throughout the campaign, earned him the award of the Distinguished Conduct Medal.

The fighting continued on this flank throughout the morning and into the afternoon. The enemy made little progress against the resistance of B and D companies but further north on their main axis *Schützenregiments* 12 and 33 made steady progress pushing behind the Dorsets. The CO of the 1/8 Lancashire Fusiliers, who had formerly served with the Dorsets, was finally forced to surrender along with most of the surviving members of his battalion, although some Fusilier stragglers joined the Dorsets.

On the Dorsets' left flank, beyond Pointe Fixe, on C Company's boundary with 7 Worcesters, Rommel was forward on the canal. He wrote:

> I now ordered 635th Engineer Battalion, which had newly been placed under command, to construct a 16-ton bridge in the sector held by Battalion Cramer near the demolished bridge at Cuinchy [Pointe Fixe].
>
> Then, under my personal direction, 20-mm AA guns and later a Panzer IV were turned on the enemy snipers [C Company], who were maintaining a most unpleasant fire from the left and picking off our men one by one. I had every house from 300 to 600 yards west of 2nd Battalion's bridging point demolished and the bushes swept with fire – after which we had some peace. I was able to see for myself how effective our fire had been when we moved back again across the canal

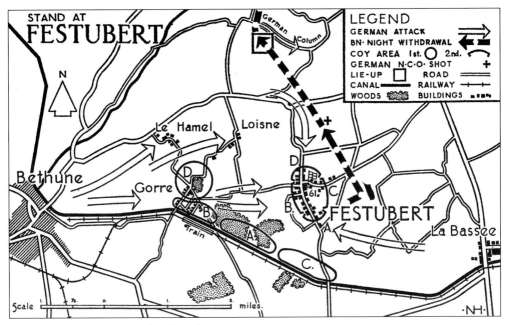

The Dorsets' stand at Festubert.

two days later. The British had installed themselves in a lock-house from which, judging by the number of empty cartridges I found there, they had maintained a steady fire in the flank of my troops. A few of our shells had wiped out the occupants of the building. Numerous blood-covered bandages and the body of a British soldier lay in the cellar.

It was quite clear that 7th Panzer Division was not having things entirely its own way near Pointe Fixe, but to the east around La Bassée the French were in action:

While these nests were being engaged, and the pioneers were con-structing a ramp on the northern bank and with great effort manoeuvring across the first pontoons, a report came in that a strong force of enemy tanks from La Bassée had attacked *Schützenregiment* 7's eastern bridgehead and thrown Battalion Cramer back across the canal. The enemy tanks, which included several British heavies [French] were now standing on the northern bank and spraying the southern bank with machine-gun and shell fire. We could hear the enemy fire a few hundred yards away.

Having borne the brunt of the preparatory attacks during 26 May and now been under direct attack all day, both 7 Worcesters and 1/8th Lancashire Fusiliers had ceased to put up organized resistance and were reduced to outposts and stragglers. Consequently, pressure now fell on 2 Dorsets:

At 1430 hours Brigade came up on the air with instructions to stand by for 'Jimmy', the code word to withdraw. Still no one knew exactly where Brigade Headquarters was, and the dispatch rider sent off on the last remaining motor-cycle to find out never returned. Three-quarters of an hour later the signal 'Jimmy' was received, together with a qualifying instruction for the Commanding Officer of 2 Dorset: 'You will hold Festubert unless attacked, when you will withdraw fighting.' The withdrawal of the 2nd Infantry Division on Estaires had already begun, and the Fifty-Fourth [2 Dorset] had been deputed to fight a rearguard action to cover the movement of the 5th Infantry Brigade and the remainder of the Division.

Rommel's bridging operations on the British left flank had been made infinitely more difficult by the presence of French tanks, which mounted forays from the outskirts of La Bassée throughout the morning. The general wrote:

> The situation was extremely critical. I drove the sappers on to their utmost speed and had the pontoons lashed roughly together, in order to get at least a few guns and the tanks across. With so many sunken and other obstacles jammed in the canal, it was impossible for the bridge to take a straight course, and its structure consequently had little strength. As the first Panzer III lumbered across, several pontoons slumped noticeably, and it was touch and go whether or not the tank would slide bodily into the canal while it was crossing. I sent off a Panzer IV fifty yards to the east along the high bank on our side of the canal, with orders to open fire immediately on the enemy tanks attacking from La Bassée. The fire of this Panzer IV brought the leading enemy tank to a halt. Shortly afterwards the Panzer III on the northern bank joined in, and a few minutes later a howitzer which had been manhandled across. This soon brought the enemy tank attack to a standstill.

Rommel specifically mentions a Panzer III above but at this stage none were in his order of battle. The possible explanations range from error through reinforcement to replacement.

With the first of Rommel's bridges capable of taking the heavier and more capable panzers, both of 5 Brigade's flanks had now collapsed with panzers leading the advance. 5 Brigade's Anti-Tank Company claimed to have knocked out twenty-one tanks during the course of the day but this figure is difficult to reconcile with figures from the 4th and 7th Panzer divisions' reports and that of 5 Panzer Brigade which joined the action later in the afternoon from reserve.

The rearward move for most of 5 Brigade was not an organized withdrawal and was well under way by mid-afternoon. The Dorsets' plan itself was simple:

A 38(t) tank crossing a pontoon bridge near La Bassée.

… all supporting arms and such mechanical transport as remained were to pull out at thirty minutes before zero, followed by the rifle companies at the appointed time. 'D' Company were to make for the north end of Festubert by a route to the north of the road from Gorre, whilst 'B' Company were to keep to the south of this road, making for the southern exits of Festubert.

D Company's withdrawal went according to plan, and they were positioned to hold the northern end of Festubert. B Company, however, was already under pressure from *Schützenregiment* 12 and was already withdrawing when the order was received. A withdrawal in contact is the most difficult phase of war and it is recorded that the company commander 'accomplished this move by splitting his company into two and making the best use he could of what cover there remained from the copses lying between him and the A Company position'. The companies moved together to Festubert. C Company had the shortest distance and brought with them the only formed remnant of 7 Worcesters: 'At 1630 hrs. 'D' Company withdrew with 2 Dorsets to FESTUBERT where they were surrounded and experienced an enemy Tank attack. Every available man came into the line, but the position was very obscure, and there was no information as to what was happening.'

The Worcesters' Battalion HQ was virtually on its own: 'Orders received to withdraw. Two Carriers remained to cover withdrawal, and later made attempts to liaise with HQ 2 Dorsetshire but found passage blocked by enemy tanks. What remained of the Battalion made for LEVANTIE.'

To return to the Dorsets, their Motor Transport Platoon was ordered back but soon after leaving Festubert they were heard to run into enemy tanks. What had happened is that they encountered elements of the 4th Panzer Division, probably the *Schützenregiment 33 Kampfgruppe* with tanks, who were now north. The war diary records 'only very few [men and vehicles] are believed to have got through'.

The Dorsets and stragglers from the other battalions were now concentrated in Festubert but they too were in a fragile state. The regimental historian recorded:

> The enemy allowed him [Colonel Stephenson] no time to assemble his forces, but, pressing relentlessly, launched an attack at about 1645 hrs. with six armoured fighting vehicles against the south-east corner of the perimeter. Regrouping was by no means complete, and elements of 'B' Company appear to have been involved in repelling this attack against 'C' Company. The enemy were driven off with the loss of one light tank.

This attack by the 7th Panzer Division was only the first against Festubert, which was a rock standing in the centre of Group Hoth's advance north.

The next attack came from the north by *Schützenregiment* 33. D Company, reinforced with Royal Warwicks and Royal Irish Fusiliers stragglers

A 37mm anti-tank gun being manhandled by its crew, as vehicles were a low priority to get across the bridges. Abandoned British carriers can be seen in the background.

Queen's Own Cameron Highlanders and French prisoners are gathered by the Germans. Panzer IIIs of 4th Panzer Division are in the background.

(remnants of Polforce) were pushed back into the village after enemy tanks bulldozed their barricade. The company's only remaining Boys anti-tank rifle was knocked out but the panzers did not follow their infantry into the village. D Company fought an 'intense close-quarter battle' with the enemy infantry that lasted for fifteen minutes before the Germans withdrew. Major Goff had received a messy and painful head wound during the withdrawal but he continued to fight his company admirably and the regimental historian is probably quite correct in saying: 'Any hesitation on his part or lack of steadfastness on the part of the company would have left that part of the perimeter wide open to penetration by the enemy.'

At around 1830 hours *Schützenregiment* 12 supported by tanks attacked from the direction of Gorre. The tanks were restricted by the boggy terrain to the west of the village and the infantry were stopped by B Company as they advanced from the copses to the south-west of Festubert. The war diary recorded '12 enemy tanks appeared about 400 yards away, only support we have is 3 A/Tank guns. 8 tanks believed to have been put out of action.'

At 1900 hours *Schützenregiment* 12 attacked again from the direction of Gorre. This time the enemy assaulted with their infantry alone and were repulsed by small-arms fire supported by the battalion's one remaining Bren carrier.

Throughout the Dorsets' stand in Festubert the Germans had attempted to unsettle the defenders:

In the general disorganization following the hurried occupation of Festubert, and the subsequent confusion caused by the four enemy attacks within about two and a half hours, some men and vehicles were lost owing to fifth-column activity. A German, disguised as a British officer, managed to circulate through the Battalion area and began issuing orders for a withdrawal to the east. In the heat of the moment these orders were not fully checked up and before this spy had been captured and summarily shot he had been able to cause a certain amount of damage.

During the afternoon of 27 May Rommel was allocated the two panzer regiments from 5 Panzer Brigade from reserve for the break-out towards Lille. Of his three formations in action General Hoth selected Rommel's as his *schwerpunkt*. Rommel's, however, was not as well developed as the others but it was the one that should be reinforced to deliver overall success. Despite delays in getting heavy equipment and panzers across the canal due to the steep ramps down to the pontoons, now with three panzer regiments coming into action by late afternoon, Rommel's advance was firmly to the north-east.

By dusk at 2100 hours such elements of 5 Brigade who could be got back had already done so and 2 Dorsets' task as rear guard had been fulfilled. Now it remained for Colonel Stephenson to extricate as much of his battalion as possible. They were reduced from nearly 1,000 strong at the beginning of the campaign to 15 officers and about 230 men plus about 60 stragglers. At 2130 hours with 7th Panzer Division's attention firmly focused on Lille, the battalion slipped out of Festubert to the east and...

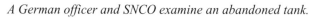

A German officer and SNCO examine an abandoned tank.

moved east for about a thousand yards and then formed up in mass with the Commanding Officer himself in the lead accompanied by the Second-in-Command and a couple of gunmen. Steve refused to delegate the responsibility for navigating his battalion over this very tricky course, avoiding all houses, woods and roads, to anyone… The course was not made any easier by constantly encountering barbed-wire fences and stumbling into and crawling out of irrigation ditches filled with warm but stagnant water. Deviations were constantly necessary… The sky all around was illuminated by burning villages and isolated farmhouses…

Three times during this withdrawal they encountered the enemy. The first occasion was after about a mile and a half, when the Colonel and his gunmen ran into a German non-commissioned officer who was advancing across country from one picket to another. The gunmen were a bit slow with their bayonets and Steve had to deal with this intruder himself, dispatching him with his revolver. It was an awkward moment: a sudden pistol shot might have had serious consequences, and everyone's heart stood still as the late lamented Heinrich's friends or subordinates started to call after him by name…and the Dorsets continued on their way, stepping as quietly as possible.

The next problem was to cross the Béthune-Estaires road several miles further on near the village of Vieille-Chapelle. On this road was a solid mass of vehicles with headlights on 'being checked past a traffic-control post at which a red light was glowing'. There was nothing for it but to lie low and, with the minutes of the short night ticking away, wait for the enemy to move on.

Another challenge was the Canal du Leie, which was reached at 0230 hours and was too deep to wade. It had to be swum with the loss of several men who drowned. It wasn't until 0500 hours that the battalion reached Estaires, their nominated rendezvous, only to find that the division had already withdrawn leaving only a French demolition party. After a three-hour halt during which they foraged for food in the abandoned French houses, they moved off again and came upon a 5 Brigade staff captain who expressed himself as being surprised to see them, the Dorsets 'having been written off as destroyed'.

Very few of 1 Camerons and 7 Worcesters made it across the canal by nightfall. In 5 Brigade only 26 officers and 263 other ranks answered roll-call, while 4 Brigade could only muster 100 all ranks. They were later joined by stragglers but even though the 'brigades' reassembled under command of the 2nd Division, as a fighting formation they were finished and the remnants were directed to Bergues and evacuation.

The 2nd Division was reconstituted and subsequently gained distinction in the fighting against the Japanese at Kohima.

Evacuation.

Battlefield Tour Information and Navigational Data

To assist visitors to the 1940 Arras battlefield in navigating their way around I have included not only the customary map coverage but GPS coordinates and the French IGN grid references, Series Bleu Sheets 2406O and 2406E. (NB: digital GPS coordinates are used, not longitude and latitude.)

   Start Point: This can be either the unlovely Douai Plain and former mining village of Vimy where the tanks assembled and orders were given, or up at the preserved trenches on Vimy Ridge where the infantry battalions dug in during the afternoon of 20 May and the night of 20/21 May.

The preserved First World War trenches adjacent to the Canadian Vimy Ridge visitor centre and car park. The trenches were used once again during the assembly phase by the DLI in May 1940.

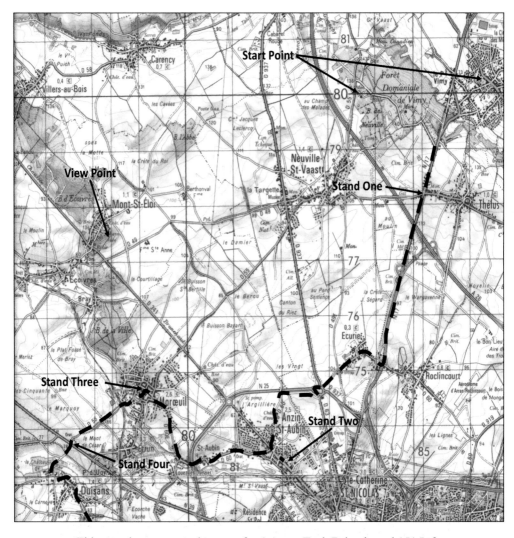

This was the concentration area for 1 Army Tank Brigade and 151 Infantry Brigade, plus troops that were regrouping from the 5th Division. In either case, return to the N17 Vimy/Arras road and head south towards Thélus.

Stand 1: Thélus Junction and Memorial GPS 50° 21' 19.9224" N and 2° 47' 22.8084", GR 851782.

This crossroads with its large memorial was the starting-point for the routes to the two columns' assembly areas and from there on to the start line. All elements of the force, less 8 DLI part of the Left Column, converged and passed through this point. 7 RTR turned right onto the outer route via Neuville-St. Vaast, which is where, to avoid the extra mileage, 8 DLI came down off Vimy Ridge to join the route.

The Left Column, both 4 RTR and 6 DLI, continued towards Arras but turning off into the village of Écurie started to transit around the city to the north and west.

Not easy to miss! The First World War memorial dominates the crossroads.

Drive through Écurie, the location of Headquarters 1 Tank Brigade. At the roundabout take the third turning signed to Arras and turn immediately right onto a minor road (D60) and follow it to the junction with the D314 in the centre of Anzin-St. Aubin.

Stand 2: Anzin-St. Aubin-Marie GPS 50° 18' 46.5768" N2° 44' 46.3056" E, GR 820734.

This village was supposedly the assembly area for the Left Column. 4 RTR paused here briefly and went on before the infantry arrived. Turn left and 200 yards further on, to the left, is a turning to the village Marie. The Marie is the hide that 'Gun Buster' describes 368 Battery using but did not meet up with the infantry who had marched straight through.

Return to the crossroads and follow the D60 to the hamlet of St. Aubin and take the D60E to Maroeuil. It was on this route down into the village that the Right Column first came under fire.

Additional Viewpoint: Mont-St. Eloi GPS 50° 35□ 05.8692□ N 2° 69□ 28.7573□ E, GR 781775.

A slight detour from the route takes one to the site of the dominating ruined abbey, from which the 12th Lancers operated until the French occupied the feature. There are truly commanding views of the whole battle area.

The ruins of Mont-St. Eloi that dominate the battle area.

The civil cemetery affords the best views and has a French 1940 memorial and graves of both British and French soldiers.

Stand 3: Maroeuil–Marie GPS 50° 19' 23.8656" N 2° 42' 20.6172" E, GR 789747.

This village was the assembly area for the Right Column where 7 RTR and 8 DLI plus various senior officers met briefly. Brigadier Churchill established his HQ 151 Brigade in the buildings around the Marie and this is where the survivors assembled after the battle.

Follow the road downhill to the bridges over the Scarpe, which is not very impressive but in 1940 was still an obstacle to tanks. This is where the first Germans were encountered.

Follow the D56 uphill, across the railway line and out into open country towards Duisans. French tanks of 3 DLM were operating across the open ground to the right.

Stand 4: Duisans Crossroads GPS 50° 18' 54.6156" N and 2° 41' 1.824" E, GR 774737.

Crossing the open country towards the roundabout on the St. Pol road/N39 is where 8 DLI met the French tanks. A few hundred yards to the north-west is the CWGC First World War cemetery. This is where the Germans were in cover and the ground from the roundabout is that covered by C Company in attacking and rounding them up.

Continue into Duisans, where the route crosses le Gy Rau watercourse and pass the château, now an educational establishment. This was 8 DLI's Main Battalion HQ run by the second-in-command Major McLaren during the battle. The village and the scrub around it were cleared by C Company.

At the junction just beyond the château, keep left and drive through the village. This is the route taken by 7 RTR. 8 DLI followed the correct route from the junction south towards Warlus.

At the end of the village fork right onto a minor road and under the railway line follow the road taken by 7 RTR and turn right to join the D60 in the hamlet of Wagnonlieu.

Stand 5: Wagnonlieu GPS 50° 28☐ 82.6626☐ N 2°71☐ 36.7894☐ E, GR 797707.

You are now back on the route of the Left Column. It was here that they ran into the rear of 4 RTR and became entangled with the head of 6 DLI. From this high ground Colonel Miller and the Durhams could see and hear 4 RTR's action going on around Achicourt. They were also shelled, so didn't dawdle!

There are now many more trees and houses on this feature that obscure the view and provide the traveller with 'cover' that those who crossed it in 1940 would not have had. A sense of openness of the terrain can, however, be gained by crossing the overpass and stopping just short of the Dainville sign.

Continue into Dainville and turn left at the traffic lights onto the D59 towards Arras. Follow the road through the much-expanded village for about 1,000 yards and turn right, still following the D59, to Achicourt. After 300 yards turn left onto the D25 towards Arras and almost immediately right onto the D60.

Stand 6: The Dainville Roundabout GPS 50° 16' 41.9232" N 2° 44' 31.8588" E. GR 816697.

Park in the area of the roundabout and walk under the road with the height barrier. The roundabout is where 4 RTR deployed to cross the start line. The level crossing that the tanks broke through is no longer there, nor is the railway line crossable. On the hillside beyond are the roads to the south-west that were

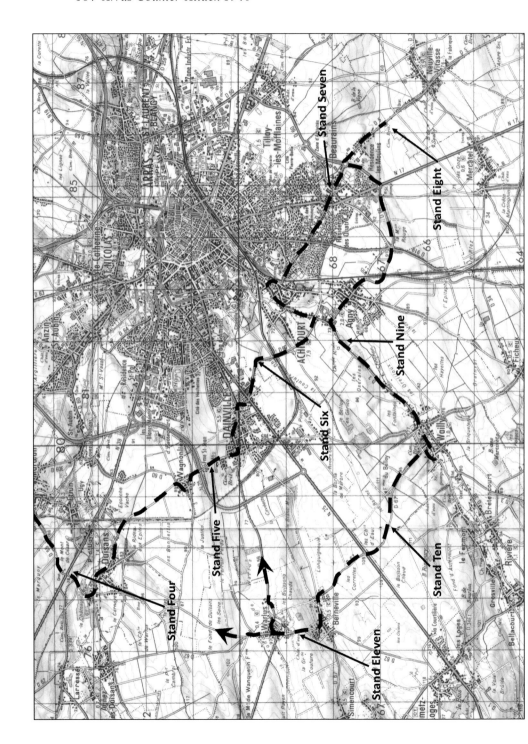

being used by the 6th Rifle Regiment and the scene of 4 RTR's 'fifteen happy minutes'.

Return to the roundabout and follow the D60 over the railway bridge. Turn left at the junction onto the D3 and follow it into Achicourt. These roads were cratered and choked with rubble by the time 6 DLI reached the village. A Company as battalion reserve was given the task of clearing a route though for the column's wheeled vehicles.

Turn right into the village square and take the turning to the left of the Marie (Rue Michel Salem). Turn right onto the D5E4 and cross the railway line. Follow the road (D5E4) through what are now the suburbs of Arras but were then open fields to the crossroads with the N17.

Stand 7: Beaurains GPS 50° 15' 48.9636" N 2° 47' 16.5192" E.

In parking by the Marie and the church just behind it you are in old Beaurains. Walking up the Rue du 1iere May to the north-east leads to C Company, 6 DLI's position but the view towards Tilloy-les-Mofflaines is now obscured by industrial units. However, on taking the Rue Pasteur and Rue Angèle Richard past the red-roofed Commonwealth War Graves Commission offices, one is into more open country; this is where D Company, 6 DLI was dug in. There are views to the south to Mercatel and the German gun lines where elements of C Squadron, 4 RTR and elements of 7 RTR fought.

Return to your car and drive on along the D5 and go straight across a large roundabout towards Neuville-Vitasse.

Stand 8: London Cemetery GPS 50° 14☐ 52.926☐ N2° 49☐ 10.8012☐ E.

Park by the cemetery (all First World War graves) or 200 yards further down at the minor crossroads. In either case you are in the centre of the area where A and D squadrons of 4 RTR came to grief from the 105mm guns on Telegraph Hill to the north and from 88mm guns up on the Neuville-Vitasse/Mercatel ridge to the south-east.

Retrace your steps back uphill to the roundabout and take the third turning onto the D60 towards Agny. Turn left at the roundabout beyond Agny onto the D3 (Rue de Pas) signed towards Wailly.

Stand 9: Agny/Wailly Road GPS 50° 26☐ 55.059☐ N 2° 75☐ 37.2809☐, GR 820679.

Stop once out in open country.

This was the main axis being used by the 6th Rifle Regiment in its transit around the south of Arras. The tanks of the two RTR regiments appeared over the ridge to the right (north). The RTR tanks crossed the road, occupied Agny and penetrated south towards Ficheux.

Follow the D3 into Wailly and at the open area take the right fork onto a village road past the church. Turn right and follow the one-way system onto the D67 (Rue de Verdun) heading out of the village uphill to the north. This is the area where Rommel encountered German troops fleeing south.

Stand 10: Ferme du Belloy GPS 50° 25☐ 30.2610☐ N 2° 69☐ 76.5295☐ E, GR 784668.

The farm itself is a working farm and can no longer welcome visitors and cars to its yard. A perfect view of the action can, however, be gained by parking in the car park adjacent to the old railway line and walking a short distance towards Arras (north-east) to the north. Rommel personally intervened in the battle to the left (north-east) of the farm near the trees.

Stand 11: Warlus GPS 50° 26☐ 97.2508☐ N 2° 66☐ 88.56763☐ E, GR 764686.

Continue downhill on the D67 crossing the N25, making a right turn followed immediately by one to the left.

The village of Berneville is the furthest point reached by elements of 8 DLI and Warlus is the village in which the battalion sheltered and resisted attack by the returning panzers until rescued by the returning French.

A good view of the area can be had by stopping by the water tower between the two villages.

From the crossroads in the centre of Warlus take the D59 towards Dainville to return to Arras or follow the D62 north out of the village and, forking right just before the cemetery (second right), to follow the Durhams' route from/back to Duisans and Maroeuil.

First Army Tank Brigade
Operation Order No. 6

21 May 40

<u>INFO</u>

1. <u>En.</u>

En have lt elms of Armd C and lt tks possibly some inf in southern outskirts of ARRAS and in the SOUTH, with colms moving towards DOULLENS.

2. <u>Own Tps</u>

Details of 48 Div are holding ARRAS and water line to the WEST probably at ÉTRUN and ACQ.

5 Div hold the line of the R SCARPE, EAST of ARRAS.

151 Inf Bde sp by 1 ARMY TK BDE and Arty 50 Div attacking round WEST and SOUTH of ARRAS.

13 Inf Bde are attacking over R SCARPE during Phase III of the attack up to the line of the rd ARRAS-CAMBRAI and R SENSÉE.

3. <u>Topographical</u>

Stream WEST of ARRAS, GRINCHORN R and COJEUL R are reported lt tk obstl. Recce should be made to confirm this.

All brs except rly br in ARRAS are blown.

INTENTION

4. 1 ARMY TK BDE will cover the attack of 151 Inf Bde round the WEST and SOUTH of ARRAS.

METHOD

5. The attack will be carried out in three phases:

Phase I	Move in f to SL which is line of rly running NE and SW through rly junc 436976.
	<u>Timing</u>: Bns cross VIMY RIDGE 1100 hrs
Phase II	Clearing area up to R COJEUL.
	<u>Timing</u>: Tks cross SL 1400 hrs
Phase III	Clearing area up to R SENSÉE
	<u>SL</u>: R COJEUL
	Timing will be issued later.

6. Fwd Bns
RIGHT 7 R TKS in sp 8 DLI
LEFT 4 R TKS in sp 6 DLI

Bn CL
RIGHT rd and rly X 412958 – VAILLY – MERCATEL – NEUVILLE-VITASSE
HENING-SUR-COJEUL – CROISILLES

LEFT rd and rly X 449982 – ACHICOURT – BEAURAINS – TILLOY-LÈS-
MOFFLAINES – WANCOURT – CHÉRISY

Bdys
RIGHT incl BOISLEUX St MARK incl CROISILLES
LEFT incl rd ARRAS – CAMBRAI
Dividing Line incl 4 TKS HENINEL 5295

7. Allotment of tks
Two sec Mark II tks from 7 R TKS to come under comd 4 R TKS

8. Inf Forming up 8 DLI MARŒUIL. 6 DLI ANZIN-ST-AUBIN
Inf adv behind tks

9. Arty One bty Fd Arty, one A/T bty in sp each 9 and 6 DLI
Sp by obsn, FOOs mov with fwd inf bn

10. Med CP at PETIT VIMY and at MARŒUIL form 1500 hrs

11. Sups Will be del to units at 1800 hrs

12. Pet PP at E of GIVENCHY. 5 Pet, 3 Disoleum lors open 1600 hrs

13. Amm AP same as PP. Opens 1600 hrs

14. A rec post will be estbl at PETIT VIMY at 1500 hrs

INTERCOMM
15. Bde HQ will remain present loc till 1400 hrs, then opens at DAINVILLE.
Subsequent movs LEFT route.

16. Wrls Silence till 1330 hrs when units net.

The 7th Panzer Division – Order of Battle
By Richard Hone

Every one of the ten panzer divisions operating in the west in the 1940 Campaign was organised differently. There were four separate basic organisations, with a varying number of battalions of tanks, infantry and artillery. The variations, however, do not stop there; vehicles, weapons and equipment varied in both type and quantity. In the case of 7th Panzer Division, for instance, being one of the most recently raised divisions, it had three panzer Battalions rather than the four in 1st–5th Panzer Divisions and the Recce Battalion's Motor Cycle Company had twice as many machine guns as any other but didn't have the normal pair of anti-tank guns. In terms of equipment the Czech 38(t) was issued in lieu of the Panzer III.

It was apparent that 7th Panzer Division was very well connected politically. Rommel's HQ had additional staff who would report to Berlin, for example an additional ADC and a liason officer who was to fly to Berlin with marked maps every evening showing the progress of the 7th Division. No wonder Rommel was a driven man.

Note that there is no signal provision in divisional HQ. This was to encourage divisional commanders to operate forward with their regiments and not hang back World War 1 style.

The combat and combat support units of Rommel's 7th Panzer Division based on the April 1940 order of Battle was:

Divisional HQ
>   Divisional HQ staff
>   Escort platoon
>   Mapping detatchment
>   Motorcycle platoon[1]
>   LuftwafferRecce flight
>   3 x Henschel HS-126 light aircraft

25th Panzer Regiment
>   Headquarters Oberst Rothenburg
>   Motorcycle section

---

1 Dispatch riders and escort duties.

Signals platoon 1 x 38(t) and 2 x 38(t) command tanks and a band
Light tank platoon 5 x 38(t)
66th Panzer Battalion[2]   Major Siekenius
I/23rd Panzer Battalion
I/25th Panzer Battalion

Each battalion had, a headquarters company of a signal platoon (1 x 38(t) and 1 x 38(t) command tanks), motor cycle (12x motor cycles and 2 x cars), flak (4 Kfz 15 with dual MG 34), light tank (5 x Pz II[3]) and engineer platoons 4 x Kfz 15 and 4 trucks (4 sections).
Two light panzer companies each of Company HQ (2 x 38(t) , Light Platoon (5 x Pz 2) and three medium platoons totalling 15 x Pz 38(t)
Medium tank company HQ 1 x Pz II and 1 x PZ VI. Light platoon (5 x Pz II), medium platoon (4 x Pz IV) and Medium tank platoon (3xPz IV)
Tank reserve detatchmen 2 x Pz II, 3 x 38(t) and 1 x Pz IV.
Panzer supply column and a workshop platoon.

7th Schützen Brigade

Headquarters[4] of a motorcycle section, signals platoon (six sections)
705th Independent Heavy Infantry Gun Company 6 x 150mm sig 33[5] 6 x Sdkfz 10 ammunition carriers.

6th Motorised Schützen Regiment   Oberst von Unger

Signals platoon and a band
One light supply column

7th Schützen Regiment   Oberst von Bismarck

Two battalions, each with a headquarters of a radio section, 2 x telephone sections, 2 x man pack radio sections.
Three schützen companies of a headquarters and 3 platoons totalling per company 18 x light MGs, 4 x heavy MGs and 3 x light 50mm mortars
Heavy Company of 6 x medium (81mm), 6 x 37mm towed anti-tank guns, light infantry guns platoon 4 x 75mm, anti tank platoon (3 x 37mm gun) and an engineer platoon.
7th Motorcycle Battalion   Major von Steinkeller
Battalion headquarters with a radio section, 2 x telephone sections, 2 x man pack radio sections.

---

2 Including an anti-aircraft Platoon – 20mm.
3 The obsolescent Panzer I and Panzer II in addition to being used as recce vehicles within the panzer battalions were employed as all purpose vehicles in one case for a battalion medical officer or converted to ambulances or ammunition carriers.
4 Very little function in battle and subsequently written out of the order of battle.
5 Mounted on Pz I chassis, with sdkfz 10 as ammunition carriers.

Two mortorcycle schützen companies each of three platoons totalling per company 18x light MGs, 4 x heavy MGs and 3 x light 50mm mortars.
Heavy company–engineer platoon, 3 x 37mm, 6 x 81 mm mortars and 2 x 75mm ligth infantry guns.

78th Artillery Regiment   Oberst Froelich
Regimental Headquarters, signal company, mapping and recconnaisance platoons, meterological section and a band.
Two Battalions, each with Battalion HQ, signals platoon, survey and forward observation platoon, three batteries, with 4 x 105mm light field howitzers[6] (total 24 guns)

37th Reconnaissance Battalion   Major Erdmann[7]
Battalion Headquarters and signals platoon (2 x Sdkfz 263).
Two armoured car companies with an HQ with 1 x Sdkfz 263 command car and 4 x Sdkfz 223 light radio cars.
Heavy Platoon 3 x Sdkfz 231 and 3 x Sdkfz 232(20mm guns).
Light Platoon 4 x Sdkfz 221 and 4 x Sdkfz 222.
Light Platoon 6 x Sdkfz 221
Motorcycle company with 18 x light MGs, 4 x heavy MGs and 3 x light 50mm mortars.
Heavy company with a engineer platoon, 2 x 75mm light infantry gun platoon.
Light supply column.

42nd Anti-Tank Battalion   Oberstleutnant Micki
Headquarters and signal platoon.
Two companies each of 12 x 37mm guns.
3rd Battery, 59th Flak Company 12 x towed 20mm.

58th Panzer Pioneer Battalion[8]   Major Binkau
Headquarters
Two motorized light pioneer company. Headquarters and three platoons.
Armoured pioneer company. Headquarters (2 x Pz II), two engineer panzer platoons (each 5 x Pz (Pioneer) I[9] and a bridging platoon (1 x Pz II and 4x Pz II bridgelayers[10])

---

6 Photographic evidence suggests that some of the guns were towed by Sdkfz 251 (Hanomag) armoured halftracks.
7 KIA 28 May. Hans von Luck took over
8 Combat Engineers
9 Two different types of 'Lardungstraeger' demolition equipment. One platoon had Sdkfz 251 Hanomag vehicles for mobility.
10 Bridge type K–weight limit 20 tons

Motorized bridge column (Type B). Two bridging platoons.
Pioneer supply column

83rd Panzer Signals Battalion[11]
Radio company
Telephone company[12]
Light supply column

59th Light Anti-Aircraft Battalion (less 3rd battery)   Major Schrader
Headquarters, signals platoon and band
Three Light Batteries 12 x 20mm (towed)

86th Luftwaffe Light Anti-Aircraft Battalion
Headquarters, signals platoon and band
Three light batteries each of 12 x 20mm mounted on Krupp 6 x 4 trucks

58th Supply and Transport Services (Battalion)
Battalion Headquarters
Six transport colums (4 x 2 trucks)[13]
Two fuel companies[14]
Three workshop companies

58th Medical Services (Battalion)
Two medical companies
Three ambulance platioons

Military Police Platoon
Field Post Services

Food Supply Unit
Bakery Company
Butchery Company[15]

1 Battery, 23 Flack Regiment
4 x 88mm dual purpose guns

---

11 No armoured units
12 A very important asset – a much underrated part of the German command
and control system
13 Lift capacity 30 tonnes each
14 50 m3 each of fuel
15 Known as the 'Sausage makers'!

Appendix III

Analysis of the Operation

As an operation, the 'Arras counter-attack' is an exemplar of much of what went wrong for the Allies in the 1940 campaign as a whole and an analysis of it could fill a volume in its own right, so a few notes regarding salient points must suffice here.

Armour

The British had pioneered the tank and had, despite military conservatism, led the way with the Mechanised Experimental Force. However, in taking the path of separate tank brigades and only belatedly starting to form an armoured division, the all-arms nature of and reports on the armoured experiments conducted by Percy Hobart on Salisbury Plain were lost to the British, although not to the Germans. Concentrating British armour in its own tank brigades rather than creating all-arms armoured formations was a mistake.

The 50th Division was mechanized but the definition of this at the time related to mobility rather than armour.

Brigadier Pope, the BEF's Armoured Advisor, wrote a memo on his return to Whitehall setting out the weakness of British armour in the late campaign:

> Will you please impress upon all concerned the following facts which we have – or at any rate I have – learned as a result of bitter experience.
>
> There must be a Commander RAC [Royal Armoured Corps] in the Field with an adequate staff to enable him to command, and he must control all movements of RAC troops as directed by the General Staff. Unless this is done, we shall continue to fritter away our tanks. We must model ourselves upon the German lines in this connection. You will be staggered to learn that 1 Army Tank Brigade marched and counter-marched the better part of 300 miles[1] to fight one action. Pratt will give you details. Similarly, 3 RTR has been thrown away. You will learn the details later.
>
> We must have thicker armour on our fighting tanks and every tank must carry a cannon. The 2-pdr is good enough now, but only just. We must mount something better and put it behind 40 to 80mm of armour.

---

1. About half this distance in reality.

All of our tanks must be mechanically simple and reliable. 75 % of our casualties have been due to mechanical failures and slow repairs.

We want the highest road speed compatible with the above. The A.12 Mk II is too slow. The A.13 is OK in this respect.

Moves by rail cannot be relied upon. The Boche can always cut the lines by air attack. All our tanks must, therefore, be capable of moving long distances at reasonably high speeds by road.

Armoured cars are invaluable for recce, and 12 L. have done marvels, but the Morris is not tactically or technically good enough. The armour must not be very thick – though the thicker the better – but the car must mount a gun: 2-pdr will do.

The Armd Reconnaissance Brigade is a wash-out. It might be able to carry out recce alone, but cannot fight a delaying action. Cruiser tanks or light tanks carrying guns are essential. I would, however, far rather have extra armoured cars.

The RAC has done extraordinarily well in the most arduous circumstances, but has suffered enormously. With suitable tanks it would have mopped up the Boche. As it is, the Boche tanks have suffered heavily.

1 Army Tank Brigade walked through everything it met, but mechanical failures have wrecked it.

I fear Cruisers Mk I and II and A.13 will prove to be too thin-skinned.

I do hope the Powers that be realize that the Boche has succeeded solely because of his mass of tanks supported by air attacks. Man for man we can beat him any day and twice a day, but dive-bombing followed by tank attack is too much on our very extended fronts.

If only 1st Armoured Division had been out here in time, it might have made all the difference.

It took until the final days of the war, four and a half years on, for the British to produce an effective gun/tank combination in the Centurion.

Tactically, despite the presence of Brigadier Pope and Colonel Miller of 6 DLI who knew from the First World War the importance of keeping up with the tanks, all-arms cooperation did not take place on 21 May. As is even noticeable in some of the early battles in Normandy, four years later the tanks and the infantry were present on the same battlefield and going in the same direction but were essentially fighting their own battles.

Infantry

Brigadier Churchill's infantry of 151 Brigade in the rush to mount the operation were the first available troops. They had not previously been in action and a year earlier they had been severely watered down by the process of doubling the TA and only brought up to strength when conscription was introduced. The eight months of the Phoney War had allowed them training time in the UK, but this was split between new recruits and weapon specialists rather on battalion and formation training. On deployment to France, labouring under III Corps had been a great distraction from preparations for battle and, of course, the Durhams had no experience of working with tanks or artillery.

Artillery

'Gun Buster's' account of the activities of 368 Battery used in preceding chapters reveals the weakness of the 1938–40 battery organization, the lack of adequate communication and just how far the Royal Regiment of Artillery was in 1940 from being the flexible, responsive and ultimately battle-winning arm of 1944/45. The story of 368 Battery also illustrates the myopia of the armoured commanders who 'charged off', and the lack of understanding of the power and use of artillery by the commanding officer of 6 DLI. No battlegroup commander of Normandy and beyond would consider any operation without having his battery commander alongside him, working communications and the guns within range. The old adage was 'no comms, no bombs' and in subsequent years when that vital radio contact could not be made, operations paused until it was re-established.

In praising the highly-effective gun line that the 7th Panzer Division had deployed on 21 May to cover the move around Arras, the British historian simply concludes that 'No comparable support could be provided by the artillery with our own attacking formations.'

All of this was, of course, exacerbated by the rushed and ad hoc nature of the operation that General Martel was required to conduct, with units from three different formations who didn't even know each other, let alone having trained together. Would more effective use of artillery on 21 May have made a difference to the outcome? Probably not in the long run, but with the tanks having knocked 7th Panzer Division off balance, timely artillery fire by the twenty-four guns of the 92nd Field Regiment on the area between Telegraph Hill and Wailly rather than on the River Cojeul bridges would have made it far more difficult for Rommel to regain control of the situation.

Command and Communications

One of the great strengths of the Germans during the 1940 campaign was their radio communications; this was in sharp contrast with the state of those of the Allies. Even allowing for degradation of command resulting from the ad hoc nature of Frankforce, German communication equipment, training, procedures and command and control structures were at virtually every level superior to those of the British in 1940 and at Arras in particular.

Communication not only enabled the Germans to pass orders quickly, but with monitoring of radio nets enhanced their senior commanders' situational awareness. This can, however, be overstated; one only has to point out that on both 20 and 21 May 1940 Rommel had to physically go back from his panzer spearheads to find his following infantry.

It would take a further two years of war before Britain could begin to match German communications, command and control and start an integration of assets into joint and all-arms forces at every level.

Air

Following on from German command and control capabilities was the effective integration with the *Luftwaffe*, the flying artillery of the blitzkrieg. The manner and speed with which all German aircraft available were tasked, launched and were in action over the fields and villages south of Arras was for the time remarkable and highly effective.

In contrast the RAF's effort had concentrated on creating a truly first-class air defence system that was comprehensively tested during the Battle of Britain. Arrangements for the support of the land battle were second-rate in terms of organization, resources and aircraft. However, with the overall situation and the move of the air component back to southern England it is hard to be critical of the lack of air support during operations around Arras on 21 May.

With blitzkrieg, the Germans had ushered in a new style of warfare that had to be understood and equipment, procedures and tactics developed before the British could think about winning battles, let alone the war.

Appendix IV

The 'Arras Counter-Attack' and the Halt Order

Rommel was the undoubted victor of the battle of 21 May 1940 in the fields and villages south and south-west of Arras. This was a victory that was in no small amount attributable to his own performance and indeed presence at the crux of the fighting. In the aftermath of the battle, his actions with the pen, however, did much to shape the course of the campaign up to the evacuation of the BEF from Dunkirk and its beaches.

Rommel, the self-publicist, could not resist writing up the action in his reports, mentioning 'hundreds of tanks' and even alluding to facing five enemy divisions. While this isn't too far off the mark (5th, 12th, 50th, Petreforce and 1 Army Tank Brigade, plus Prioux's Corps), his reporting painted these up as being full divisions in the offensive, which equated to an operational-level counter-stroke rather than a tactical clearance of the area south of Arras. Consequently, there was a gross overreaction from those remote from the reality of the battlefield itself. The disconnect between panic in Berlin, largely caused by reports sent direct to *OKW*, and events in northern France is exemplified by an entry in the neighbouring *Panzer Corps Reinhart*'s war diary late on the evening of 21 May:

> ...today is marked by exaggeration and partly false news and reports. There is talk of a breakthrough by an enemy formation with about fifty panzers that is reputed to be advancing towards Doullens. This bit of news turns out to be completely false. All other messages about the... counter-attack are also exaggerated.

The officers of the *Panzerwaffe* were not concerned; with far more accurate reports on the condition of the Allied troops who were 'everywhere falling back', the panzer corps commanders were ready to resume operations. They wanted to capitalize on their strike to the sea by not just enveloping but surrounding the BEF by cutting them off from the Channel ports. This would condemn the northern Allied armies to destruction in what was already referred to as the Flanders Pocket.

However, with, for example, the near success of Colonel De Gaulle's attack some days earlier, the Germans had, as evidenced by the increasing timidity both in Berlin and in the upper echelons of the forces in the field, increasingly feared the inevitability of a major Allied counterstroke. Based on Rommel's reports, which shot up the chain of command, this appeared to most, from von Kleist upwards, to have been the counterstroke or at the very least a serious manifestation of the threat.

Throughout the night of 21/22 May, Hitler had aides ring Army Group A for immediate situation reports on the 'Arras crisis' and even dispatched Keitel, chief of staff of the *OKW*, to northern France to deal with the crisis and reinforce orders to halt the advance and to concentrate on 'resolving the situation at Arras'. This alone had an impact on events as far as the completeness of the German victory in northern France is concerned. The 10th Panzer Division was in position to advance along the – at this stage – barely-defended coast, taking Boulogne, Calais and Dunkirk and thus cutting off the BEF from the possibility of evacuation. This first pause in German operations to focus on Arras in the wake of the 21st arguably on its own saved the BEF but was followed by the infamous 'Halt Order' of 24 May 1940.

The Halt Order

The 'Arras counter-attack' and fear of further such Allied operations have often been cited as the cause of the *OKW* issuing another Halt Order; an order that gave breathing space for the BEF to withdraw to Dunkirk and evacuation. This, however, is not the only reason advanced for Hitler's order. Briefly these are as follows:

> **Allied Counter-Offensive:** Despite mounting evidence that the Allies lacked the capacity and even the will to conduct operational-level counterstrokes, Hitler and von Rundstedt steadfastly believed that such an operation would be mounted. As already mentioned, the 'Arras counter-attack' had put flesh on the bones of what had previously been only a growing concern.

> **Conserving the *Panzerwaffe*:** The panzer divisions, while not exactly bearing the brunt of the fighting since 10 May, had suffered significant vehicle casualties from enemy action and breakdown. The envelopment and eventual destruction of the armies in the north, it was argued, would only be the first phase, with the remainder of the French army to defeat in a very large country. Therefore time to regroup, rest, replenish and repair the *Panzerwaffe* was necessary.

> **Ground Considerations:** Many of the German commanders had experience of Flanders during the First World War and believed that the coastal plain was unsuitable for tanks, being not only boggy but criss-crossed by drainage ditches and canals, which would have made any advance time-consuming. Up until 24 May the ground was firm following a protracted warm, dry period.

These were relatively straightforward military considerations that commanders and staffs would routinely discuss and come to a conclusion but there are more, some of which amount to little more than excuses. These were advanced, both at the time and since, as being contributory factors to the Halt Order. They are as follows:

The *Luftwaffe*: A bombastic Göring, commander-in-chief of the *Luftwaffe*, told the Führer that 'the *Luftwaffe* can give the English the coup de grâce' on their own. This statement was widely and immediately derided. Jodl said 'He is shouting his mouth off again' and a significantly large proportion of the *Luftwaffe* commanders and staff said it was impossible. However, from Hitler's perspective, it at least offered the possibility of maintaining pressure on the evacuation during the period of the Halt.

Naval Understanding: It has been claimed that a lack of understanding of amphibious capability in Berlin led to an underestimation of the British capacity to evacuate the BEF 'trapped' in the Flanders Pocket.

Letting the British go: Hitler, in the aftermath of the campaign, said on several occasions that he let the British go and reiterated it in his last political testament during the dying days of the war. Hitler indeed had a preference for the English in an alliance that would see the two 'Germanic nations' dividing the world between them. The corollary of this is said to be that in halting the panzers on 24 May he did not wish to defeat them so badly that a political accord of some kind would be precluded. With the military situation, as well as that in Churchill's own Cabinet room, this was not an entirely unreasonable hope. Matters were, however, rarely straightforward with Hitler and to balance these claims the Führer is on record as saying that he wanted 'the SS to participate in the final annihilation of the English' and Göring said 'The Führer wants them to be taught a lesson that they won't easily forget!' There are frequently two sides of Hitler to be found.

With all these factors playing a greater or lesser role in Hitler's fateful halt decision, one that allowed the BEF to slip away, it is plain to see that the 'Arras counter-attack' for all its faults in conception and execution was indeed significantly instrumental in saving the BEF. It may, however, be going a little too far to say that the time bought by the timely shock to the German high command, administered by the mixed force on 21 May, allowed not only the evacuation but for Churchill to make the prospect of negotiations through the 'good offices' of Mussolini impossible to countenance across both the Cabinet table and the nation.

Index